C A Jackson BA. BSc.,
Reader. St. Laurence York.
YORK MINSTER 30TH DEC. 1981

PRAYERS THAT LIVE

FRANK COLQU
Vice-Dean of
life was spent in
Vicar of Wallin
lor of Southwa
Ordination Co

His many b ... Contemporary *Parish Prayers* and *Hymns That Live*. He is also editor of the revised edition of the BBC service book *New Every Morning*.

Frank Colquhoun

PRAYERS THAT LIVE

TRIANGLE

SPCK

First published 1981
Triangle
SPCK
Holy Trinity Church
Marylebone Road
London NW1 4DU

Reproduced, printed and bound in Great Britain by
Hazell Watson & Viney Ltd, Aylesbury, Bucks

ISBN 0 281 03815 5

To my wife

Contents

III THE PATTERN PRAYER

Abbreviations

ASB	Alternative Service Book, 1980
BCP	Book of Common Prayer, 1662
AV	Authorized Version of the Bible, 1611
GNB	Good News Bible, 1976
NEB	New English Bible, 1961 and 1970
NIV	New International Version of the Bible, 1974
RSV	Revised Standard Version of the Bible, 1952, 1971

Acknowledgements

Extracts from the Authorized King James Version of the Bible and the Book of Common Prayer of 1662, which are Crown Copyright, are reproduced with permission.

Extracts from the Revised Standard Version of the Bible, copyrighted 1946 and 1952 by the Division of Christian Education of the National Council of the Churches of Christ in the USA, are reproduced with permission.

Extracts from the New English Bible, second edition © 1970, are reproduced by permission of Oxford and Cambridge University Presses.

Extracts from the New International Version of the Bible, copyright © the New York International Bible Society, are reproduced by permission of Hodder & Stoughton.

Extracts from the Good News Bible – New Testament, copyright © American Bible Society 1966, 1971, 1976, are reproduced by permission of the British and Foreign Bible Society.

Thanks are due to Donald Coggan for permission to quote from his *The Prayers of the New Testament*, published by Hodder & Stoughton.

Preface

The short studies that make up this book offer a devotional commentary on some well known prayers, with a view to making them more meaningful to those who use them. The prayers selected vary considerably as regards their age, origin, style and themes; but in general it can be claimed, I think, that they are prayers that 'live': not only in the sense that they have stood the test of time but in the more personal sense that they continue to touch our lives at a deep level. Obviously not all of them have the same appeal, or will appeal to the same people, for we are not all made alike. Nevertheless, as I have endeavoured to show, there is in each of them something of spiritual worth that can help us in our approach to God and bring us into closer fellowship with him.

The studies are in three sections. The first includes a varied selection of favourite prayers from early times to the present century. The reflections and comments offered here are largely my own, as I have failed to find any literature dealing in detail with prayers of this kind.

The situation is different when it comes to the second section, which comprises prayers from the Book of Common Prayer. Numerous works of reference are available in this field, and allusion is made to some of these in the short note at the beginning of the section. In the main the prayers chosen for study are the more familiar ones from Morning and Evening Prayer and the Holy Communion, with a representative group of collects covering the principal seasons and festivals of the Church's year.

I hope these studies may appeal particularly to those who, like myself, have been brought up on the Prayer Book and to whom many of its prayers are devotional treasures. Happily, the majority of these prayers find a place, in a modified form, in the Alternative Service Book.

In the third section I offer a series of simple and straightforward studies in the Lord's Prayer. Nothing new can be said about this greatest of prayers. All the same, if we are to learn what prayer really means we need constantly to go back to the teaching of Jesus, to reflect upon the familiar words he gave us, and to see their relevance to our own time, our own world, and our own lives.

Finally I wish to express my thanks to Miss Myrtle Powley, Editor of Triangle Books, for her assistance and advice in preparing this book for publication.

FRANK COLQUHOUN

One

PRAYERS ACROSS THE CENTURIES

A Prayer after Saint Augustine

> *Eternal God, who art the light of the minds that know thee, the joy of the hearts that love thee, and the strength of the wills that serve thee: Grant us so to know thee that we may truly love thee, and so to love thee that we may fully serve thee, whom to serve is perfect freedom, in Jesus Christ our Lord.*

Robert Louis Stevenson in his *Travels with a Donkey in the Cevennes* tells how, as he set off on his journey early one morning, he was overtaken by a godly old man (a Plymouth Brother, as it turned out) who walked beside him and chatted as they went.

> It was not much past six; and for healthy people who have slept enough, that is an hour of expansion and of open and trustful talk.
>
> *'Connaissez-vous le Seigneur?'* he said at length.
>
> I asked him what Seigneur he meant; but he only repeated the question with more emphasis and a look in his eyes denoting hope and interest.
>
> 'Ah,' said I, pointing upwards, 'I understand you now. Yes, I know Him; He is the best of acquaintances.'
>
> The old man said he was delighted. 'Hold,' he added, striking his bosom; 'it makes me happy here.'

Knowing the Lord is the starting point of this prayer, which is freely adapted from a passage in the *Meditations* of St Augustine (354–430). Quite clearly it falls into two sections. The first provides a kind of prelude; the second constitutes the prayer itself. In its entirety it is occupied with three themes: knowing God, loving him, and serving him.

God is *the light of the minds* of those who *know* him. Without that light our minds are darkened. We may have knowledge of a thousand and one things and be 'educated' to the highest possible level; but without the knowledge of God we are not spiritually enlightened. Moreover, that knowledge cannot be acquired by our own efforts. To Job's question, 'Canst thou by searching find out God?' (Job 11.7 AV), the answer is, 'No'. The knowledge of God is not a human discovery. It is a divine disclosure. It is the light of revelation; and that light shines for us in its fullness in the face (i.e. the person) of Jesus Christ (2 Corinthians 4.6).

Again, God is *the joy of the hearts* of those who *love* him. To love God is to find the secret of joy which is deep and abiding because it is inward and spiritual. Ordinary human happiness, as the word itself denotes (it comes from 'hap', to chance or happen), depends on outward events, on the changing and capricious circumstances of life. Christian joy, the joy of the Christian believer, is independent of circumstances and finds its source in the unchanging God.

And God, who enlightens the minds of those who know him and rejoices the hearts of those who love him, also strengthens *the wills* of those who *serve* him. He gives them courage and resolution to be constant in his service and remain faithful to the end.

All this forms the prelude to the prayer itself. It looks at the three themes of knowledge, love and service, separately and independently. The prayer that follows links them together in a progressive order and makes them cohere. Hence the first petition is: *Grant us so to know thee that we may truly love thee.* We cannot be content with a superficial knowledge of God or with a love that is not strong and true.

The prayer echoes the words of the Benediction in the BCP (see p. 92) and the prayer of St Richard (p. 11) in thus relating our knowledge of God to our love for him. It is a matter of simple logic. We cannot love God if we do not know him. Conversely, we cannot know God without loving him – that is, if we know him as he is revealed to us in Jesus Christ. A further bit of logic follows. The deeper our knowledge of God, the stronger will be our love for him. To know him well is to love him truly.

That is our next concern: grant us *so to love thee that we may fully serve thee*. Our service is the evidence and expression of our love for God. Failure to serve him 'fully' – that is, to the full extent of our ability and opportunity – is due in all likelihood to the paucity of our love. The fire of devotion has burned low within our souls. We need the flame of sacred love to be rekindled on the mean altar of our hearts, so that we may render more worthy service to him *whom to serve is perfect freedom*.

This latter phrase occurs in almost similar form in the second collect of Morning Prayer and is likewise derived from Augustine: 'whose service is perfect freedom'. The Latin *cui servire regnare est* is literally 'whom to serve is to reign'. To be the servants of God is to enjoy sovereign freedom, paradoxical as it may sound. Can a servant be free? It is nevertheless true in this case. God made us for himself and for his service. Hence only in his service do we fulfil the purpose of our creation and become fully human. And therefore only in his service are we truly free: free from the servitude of sin, free to obey the will of God in holiness and righteousness.

George Matheson (1842–1906) expresses this truth superbly in his hymn, 'Make me a captive, Lord, And then I shall be free'. The second verse runs:

> My heart is weak and poor
> Until it master find;
> It has no spring of action sure –
> It varies with the wind.
> It cannot freely move
> Till thou hast wrought its chain;
> Enslave it with thy matchless love,
> And deathless it shall reign.

Called to Serve

Remember, O Lord, what thou hast wrought in us, and not what we deserve; and as thou hast called us to thy service, make us worthy of our calling; through Jesus Christ our Lord.

We owe our translation of this ancient collect from the Leonine Sacramentary to Dr J. Armitage Robinson (1858–1933), sometime Dean of Westminster and a renowned patristic scholar. It found its way into the Occasional Prayers of the 1928 Prayer Book and as a result it has become very widely known.

Short and simple as it is, like many of the old collects it says quite a lot in a very little space. However, it is unlike most collects in that it has no preamble or descriptive clause but plunges straight away into prayer. It contains two petitions, the first of which prepares the way for the second.

Remember, O Lord, what thou hast wrought in us, and not what we deserve. What has God wrought in us? Everything in us that is good and true, strong and holy. A couple of sentences in St Paul's letter to the Philippian Christians provides a commentary. At the outset of the letter he expresses his confidence 'that he who began a good work in you will carry it on to completion until the day of Christ Jesus' (1.6 NIV); and in the next chapter, after urging them to work out their salvation with fear and trembling, he explains: 'for it is God who works in you to will and do what pleases him' (2.12, 13 NIV).

God's work in us is progressive. It is begun, continued, and ended in him through his Holy Spirit dwelling in our hearts.

And every virtue we possess,
And every victory won,

And every thought of holiness,
Are his alone.

It is this that we ask the Lord to 'remember': what he has done for us, and is doing in us day by day – not what we deserve. He deals with us in grace. He gives us everything. We deserve nothing. To quote a phrase from Pope John's *Journal of a Soul*, this is 'the humble prayer of a Christian who . . . knows the magnitude of his own unworthiness, but knows even better the greater magnitude of the Lord's mercy'.

Against this background we present the second petition: *as thou hast called us to thy service, make us worthy of our calling*. Undeserving and unworthy as we are, God has called us to his service; and what he has wrought in us equips us for that service.

The petition, then, is about vocation and ministry, like the second of the Good Friday collects in which we pray that every member of the Church, in his vocation and ministry, may 'truly and godly serve' the Lord.

We are called to serve – every one of us. We all have a vocation to fulfil, a ministry to exercise; and this applies to clergy and laity alike. To draw too sharp a distinction between them is a mistake from the biblical point of view. The New Testament teaches the priesthood of all believers, or as we might better express it, the priesthood of the whole Church (1 Peter 2.5, 9). We may distinguish between the ordained priesthood and the lay priesthood; but it is essentially one priesthood, derived from the priesthood of Christ himself.

No one in modern times felt more keenly about this than the missionary statesman and theologian, Max Warren (1904–77). He recognized a differentiation of *function* within the totality of God's people, but not a hierarchy of *status*. Expressing his conviction as an evangelical churchman he wrote:

> The whole *Laos* exists to be God's priest for the world, God's witness in the world, God's messenger to the world . . . I believe that in our particular witness to the nature of the Church we have the key to open the door to a new evangelistic enterprise. We are not afraid of the ordinary man. We are not separated from him by exaggerated doctrines of the significance of an earthly priesthood. Indeed

> we hold firmly to the belief that in the solemn activity of introducing men and women to God as their Creator, Judge and Saviour, the layman can play as direct a part as any ordained priest.[1]

Not many years ago, such a concept would have been regarded as revolutionary and partisan. Happily, it is a truth which is now receiving due recognition in all Christian communions.

Called to serve. This is what the collect is basically about. What matters for us all is that we should seek to be worthy of our calling. And not only worthy of our calling, but more worthy of him who has called us to his service. We cannot make ourselves worthy. That is why we ask the Lord to do it. Worthy, and yet always unworthy – such is our position. For when we have carried out all our Master's orders, we are bound to acknowledge, 'We are unworthy servants; we have only done what was our duty' (Luke 17.10).

Note

[1]F. W. Dillistone, *Into All the World* (Hodder & Stoughton, 1980), pp. 62–3.

A Prayer ascribed to Saint Francis

Lord, make us instruments of thy peace. Where there is hatred, let us sow love; where there is injury, pardon; where there is discord, union; where there is doubt, faith; where there is despair, hope; where there is darkness, light; where there is sadness, joy.

Traditionally this prayer has always been ascribed to St Francis of Assisi (1181–1226), and no doubt the tradition will continue. But modern research has failed to find any historical link between the prayer and St Francis, so that its authorship is in considerable doubt. However, it can at least be claimed that the prayer reflects the spirit of St Francis, and with that we must be content.

The phrase with which the prayer begins, *Lord, make us instruments of thy peace*, is the key to all that follows. Instruments of God's peace! It is an arresting expression. There are things which the Lord wants done in the world for which he requires our co-operation, and without which he is limited. The eminent surgeon, Sir Frederick Treves, was once involved in a railway accident in which many were seriously injured. As he walked up and down assisting people in the wreckage, he was heard to exclaim, 'Oh, if only I had my instruments!'

The Church is the instrument through which God accomplishes his purposes and furthers his will on earth. We cannot deny, of course, that in his sovereign wisdom and power he can make use of other means to carry out his designs. Nevertheless it remains true that the Church is the supreme agency of his kingdom in the world. St Paul's concept of the Church as the Spirit-filled Body of Christ illustrates this truth. It is through the different members of the Body, with their different gifts, that he, the Head, continues his work.

We are the Body of Christ. As such we are his instruments, both corporately and individually. We are instruments of his peace.

Peace is a biblical word rich in meaning. It derives from the Hebrew *shalom*, which is a strongly positive concept. It denotes harmony, wholeness, well-being – all that makes for the good of human life and society. It is of this peace that we are to be the instruments. In his Sermon on the Mount Jesus said, 'Blessed are the peacemakers'. In using that term he was not talking of people with a peaceful disposition or with peaceful intentions. He was talking of peace*makers*: those who create peace and who are therefore instruments of peace in a world where true peace is in tragically short supply.

The prayer takes a realistic view of the sort of world in which we live. It is a world where there is *hatred*: bitterness, strife, bloodshed; a world where people suffer *injury* through injustice and oppression; a world where *discord* reigns within families, communities, churches, nations; a world where *doubt* of God's love and mercy and very existence leads to *despair*, the despair of those for whom life has no meaning, no purpose, no future; so there is *darkness* of the mind and spirit, and with it *sadness* of heart.

In such a situation we pray that the Lord may make us instruments of his peace. We are asking him to use us in a ministry of compassion and healing, of reconciliation and renewal, of encouragement and consolation. We can exercise such a ministry only by being *his* instruments and bringing into the life of mankind the positive qualities detailed in the prayer. And the first and greatest of these is *love*. Moreover let us not forget that what an instrument accomplishes depends upon the hand that holds it.

St Francis, with whom this prayer is so closely associated, was an instrument of peace in God's hand. His life exemplifies and illustrates the meaning of the prayer. A further prayer, also commonly ascribed to him, is often added to this, in order to round it off. It provides a suitable finish to this reflection as well:

> Grant that we may seek not so much to be consoled, as to console; to be understood, as to understand; to be loved, as to love.
>
> For it is in giving we receive, in pardoning we are pardoned, in dying we are born to life eternal.

The Prayer of Saint Richard of Chichester

Thanks be to thee, our Lord Jesus Christ, for all the benefits which thou hast given us, for all the pains and insults which thou has borne for us.

O merciful Redeemer, Friend and Brother, may we know thee more clearly, love thee more dearly, and follow thee more nearly.

St Richard of Chichester, who died at Dover on 3 April 1253, at the age of fifty-six, was one of the most loved and respected bishops of his day. The son of a Worcestershire farmer, he began life as a ploughboy, but eventually succeeded in securing a place at Oxford, where he distinguished himself as a scholar. Later he became Chancellor of the University. He was not ordained till after the age of forty, yet within a year or two he was elected Bishop of Chichester in 1244.

In an age when many abuses abounded in the Church his episcopate of some nine years set a pattern of reforming zeal, pastoral care and simplicity of life which greatly endeared him to his people. His tomb is to be seen in Chichester Cathedral. He was canonized in 1262. He is the last of the 'saints' to find a place in the Calendar of the BCP.

It seems that his prayer was originally written in the singular. It is reproduced here (as is commonly done) in the plural form, to give it a corporate character. It has become even more widely known in recent years through its inclusion in the musical 'Godspell', with the additional ending 'day by day'.

The prayer has the distinction of beginning on a note of thanksgiving. Comparatively few familiar prayers begin in this way. The prayer is also unusual in being addressed directly to *our Lord Jesus Christ*. The thanksgiving is *for all the benefits* which he has bestowed upon us, and most especially for the benefits of his passion. The benefits flow from the passion. Everything else that he has given us is the result of *all the pains and insults* he endured for us when he died for our salvation.

This then is a prayer to be said beneath the cross of Jesus, and to be said not only with gratitude but with humility and penitence. It is the prayer of a sinner who acknowledges his eternal indebtedness to Jesus Christ: who knows that he has been bought with a price.

O most merciful Redeemer, Friend, and Brother – three wonderful titles which form the heart of the prayer. As *Redeemer*, Jesus is our 'strong Deliverer', the one who has rescued us – and rescues us – from the slavery of sin. The word links up this part of the prayer with the thanksgiving which precedes it. We cannot think of our redemption in Christ apart from what it cost him: the giving of his life for the sin of the world.

Our Redeemer is also our *Friend*. That actual word is not used of Jesus in the New Testament (though his critics called him contemptuously 'the friend of sinners'), but the idea is certainly there. For what is the essence of friendship? It is love – love that is deep, strong, and faithful; and such is the love of Christ for us. Moreover he declared, 'I have called you friends.' Since he calls us *his* friends we may rightly call him ours – so long as we do what he commands us (John 15.14, 15).

Jesus is also our *Brother*. A brother is more than a friend. He is a kinsman, a member of the same family. Jesus declared that those who do the will of his Father are his brothers (Matthew 12.49, 50). So he is not ashamed to call *us* his brothers, as the writer to the Hebrews says. He is our Elder Brother, who having shared our human life, has full understanding of our human needs (Hebrews 2.14–18).

The titles we have looked at provide the link with the prayer that follows. It is not difficult to discern a progression in the three petitions: *May we know thee more clearly, love thee more dearly, and follow thee more nearly*.

To *know* Christ is the beginning: for us, as it was for the first disciples. What is meant is a personal, first-hand knowledge. To know *about* our Lord is not enough. To be content with the knowledge we already have is also not enough. Our prayer is that we may know him more clearly, and gain a deeper insight into who he is and what he can mean to us as our risen Lord. 'That I may know him and the power of his resurrection!' was St Paul's fervent longing. 'Let us know, let us press on to know the Lord!' cried the prophet Hosea (6.3). Such is the aspiration expressed in this petition of St Richard's prayer.

Our deepening knowledge of Christ can have only one consequence. It is that we come to *love* him more dearly. To grow in the knowledge of Christ is to grow in the love of Christ, for it is to learn something more of what he has done for us. The Cross is 'the measure and the pledge of love' – Christ's love for us; and we love him because he first loved us.

The final petition, that we may *follow* him more nearly, is the practical outcome. To follow Christ is to translate our knowledge and love of him into action. It is to walk in his steps, to obey his commands, to imitate his example. The pattern he set his disciples was this: 'The Son of Man came to serve, and to give his life as a ransom for many.'

To follow him more nearly does not simply mean becoming more religious. It means taking up our cross and treading with him the way of sacrificial love. A hard way? Yes indeed. But St Richard of Chichester trod that way himself.

The Way, the Truth, and the Life

O Lord Jesus Christ, who art the way, the truth, and the life, suffer us not at any time to stray from thee, who art the way; nor to distrust thy promises, who art the truth; nor to rest in any other thing than thee, who art the life; for thou hast taught us what to believe, what to do, and wherein to take our rest.

It was the question of a doubting man, remarks Dr William Barclay, which provoked one of the greatest things that Jesus ever said. He was referring to our Lord's response to Thomas's inquiry, 'Lord, we do not know where you are going; how can we know the way?' His reply was, 'I am the way, the truth, and the life; no one comes to the Father, but by me' (John 14.5, 6).

The prayer we are looking at is built around these words of Jesus. It is abridged from the first section of a long prayer by Erasmus (1466–1536), the most distinguished Christian scholar of his day, whose theological writings – and in particular his edition of the Greek New Testament, 1516, with his Latin translation – profoundly influenced the course of the Reformation. The prayer is addressed *ad Filium*, that is, to God the Son, as the opening words make clear.

When Jesus said to Thomas, 'I am the way . . . no one comes to the Father but by me', he was declaring in the plainest possible manner that he himself is the road by which we travel to God. He does not simply tell us the way, or point us the way. He *is* the way. And as William Temple remarks, we do not have to find its starting point. It starts here, just where we are.

The prayer assumes that we have indeed started. Its concern is that, having started, we should keep to the way – that is, to Jesus – and not *stray* from him or get side-tracked. The danger is one that we cannot ignore. 'The world, the flesh, and Satan dwell around the path I tread', as the hymn puts it, and we need to watch our steps. In Bunyan's allegory we learn that the pilgrims Christian and Hopeful strayed from the way into By-path Meadow and as a result found themselves incarcerated in Doubting Castle.

Now Doubting Castle is a most dismal abode for followers of the Way; and so our prayer to him continues: *nor* (suffer us) *to distrust thy promises, who art the truth*. Jesus is the truth personified. He embodies the truth he proclaimed; and that means we learn the truth not only by listening to him but also by looking at him. His life and deeds, his character and example, are as much a revelation of the truth as his teaching. 'He who has seen me,' he told Philip in the same discourse, 'has seen the Father' (John 14.9; cf. 1.18).

If we accept that claim, we should have no difficulty in trusting his promises. Remember, it was Christian's discovery of the key called Promise which eventually enabled the unhappy pilgrims to open the door of their prison and escape from the clutches of Giant Despair. The same key is at every believer's disposal. It is folly to distrust Christ's promises. 'This is the victory that overcomes the world, even our faith' (1 John 5.4) – faith in him who is the Truth and whose word is wholly trustworthy. As Charles Wesley wrote:

> Faith, mighty faith, the promise sees,
> And looks to that alone;
> Laughs at impossibilities,
> And cries, It shall be done!

The element of faith also enters into the third petition. Jesus is not only the way to God and the ultimate truth about him. He is also the life, and we therefore pray that we may *rest* our trust in him – in him and in nothing else – and so possess the life he came to bring us, without which we are spiritually dead.

Jesus called it 'eternal life'. Strictly speaking, 'eternal' is a property which belongs to God alone. Eternal life, therefore, is not endless existence but life of a distinctive quality, a divine quality – nothing less than the life of God himself. That life belongs to all who repose their faith in Christ. In the words of the apostle John: 'God has given us eternal life, and this life is found in his Son. He who possesses the Son has life indeed; he who does not possess the Son of God has not that life' (1 John 5.11, 12 NEB).

Jesus Christ is the Way to God, the Truth incarnate, the Life eternal. Erasmus fashioned these themes into a prayer. A century earlier Thomas à Kempis had reflected on them in his *Imitation of Christ*:

> 'I am the Way, the Truth, and the Life.' Without the Way there is no going; without the Truth there is no knowing; without the Life there is no living. I am the Way which you must follow, the Truth which you must believe, the Life for which you must hope.

A Prayer of Saint Ignatius Loyola

Teach us, good Lord, to serve thee as thou deservest: to give and not to count the cost; to fight and not to heed the wounds; to toil and not to seek for rest; to labour and not to ask for any reward, save that of knowing that we do thy will; through Jesus Christ our Lord.

What does it mean to serve God as he deserves? Few of us would pretend that we serve him in any such way. Our service falls far short of what God deserves or desires. It is more likely to be in accordance with what we ourselves find most fitting, or even most convenient. Yet again and again we pray, *Teach us, good Lord, to serve thee as thou deservest.*

It was St Ignatius of Loyola (1491–1556) who gave us the prayer. And he had the right to do so, for the words reflect his own passionate devotion to the Lord. The son of a noble Spanish family, he early fulfilled his ambition to be a soldier; but when at the age of thirty he was converted he caught a vision of a new pattern of life in the service of Christ. Thenceforward his life was dedicated to that service, and to the founding of the Order of the Society of Jesus.

We look at the prayer and discover that to serve the Lord as he deserves is to serve him with uncalculating generosity: *to give and not to count the cost*. The phrase means, of course, to give regardless of the cost. There is a sense in which, as Jesus warned us, we ought not to become his disciples without first counting the cost. The two brief parables of the man planning to build a tower and the king preparing to go to war illustrate this (Luke 14.27–33). Before saying 'Yes' to Jesus, we must be ready to pay the price. But once having committed ourselves, there must be no half measures, no holding back. We must be ready to give all we have, like the man who found the pearl of great price (Matthew 13.45–6). There is no such thing as being a Christian on the cheap.

God's service not only demands uncalculating generosity. It also deserves unflinching courage: *to fight and not to heed the wounds*. To be a Christian is to be on active service for the Lord. There are battles to be fought and foes to be overcome. St Ignatius knew that well enough. Although he abandoned his soldier's calling, he always remained a soldier at heart. 'The soldier's instincts of loyalty, obedience and courage he never lost,' wrote Alick Bouquet, 'but when he became the Cavalier of Christ he consecrated them all to Christ's Service.'[1]

It is not surprising, then, that he thought of Christ's service in military terms. He had enlisted, as he declared, under the banner of 'the supreme Captain-General, Christ our Lord'. He was prepared to endure hardship as a good soldier of Christ (2 Timothy 2.3), and he certainly did not expect to emerge from the fight without a few wounds. Nor should we. Christianity is not a spiritual picnic. It is a holy war against sin, the world, and the devil. To keep fighting manfully to the end calls for courage and resolution.

Again, God's service requires unremitting endeavour: *to toil and not to seek for rest*. The world being the sort of place it is, there is a lot of hard work to be done by the servants of Christ. And there is work for everyone. We have a quaint way of speaking of certain church members as 'Christian workers', as though the rest were Christian shirkers. It is a false distinction. 'Go work today in my vineyard', is Christ's word to us all. Perhaps to some of us he is saying, 'Why do you stand here all the day idle?'

We must be ready to toil and not to seek for rest. But that does not mean we should never rest. The point is that we should not *seek* for rest, as though that were our primary aim. Work must have the priority. At the same time we must take advantage of life's resting places, so that we may renew our strength; and in the midst of our toils we must seek to cultivate a spirit of inner tranquillity. This is what St Augustine meant by his words, *Semper agens, semper quietus* – always doing, always still.

Finally, God's service deserves our undivided loyalty: *to labour and not to ask for any reward, save that of knowing that we do thy will*. Such a petition rules out any idea of self-interest or self-pleasing. We do not engage in the service of Christ for what we can get out of it or to gain a special place in heaven. Our single desire is to do the Master's will.

Yet did not our Lord promise that the good and faithful servant would be rewarded? Most certainly he did, and doubtless that promise will be fulfilled. But the matter of reward is *his* concern, not ours. The motives that prompt our service are different: our love for Christ, our obedience to his word, our gratitude for all that he has done for us, and the sheer privilege of serving and furthering his kingdom in the world. The highest motive of all is expressed in the words which St Ignatius chose as the motto of his Order: *Ad majorem Dei gloriam*: For the greater glory of God.

Note

[1] *A People's Book of Saints* (Longmans Green, 1936), p. 256.

God be in my Head

God be in my head, and in my understanding;
God be in my eyes, and in my looking;
God be in my mouth, and in my speaking;
God be in my heart, and in my thinking;
God be at my end, and at my departing.

This prayer is usually ascribed to a Sarum Primer of 1558, but in fact it is of slightly earlier origin. It is found on the title page of a Book of Hours dated 1514, in the library of Clare College, Cambridge. It appears to have been used in the sixteenth century as a private prayer before the daily offices.

Nowadays we are inclined to regard it as a hymn rather than as a prayer, as it is more commonly sung than said. It first appeared as a hymn in the *Oxford Hymn Book*, 1908. Doubtless its popularity as a hymn owes much to the delightful setting by Sir Walford Davies.

Whether said or sung, the prayer is a devotional gem. It commends itself by its directness, simplicity, and brevity. It is the prayer of a person who humbly recognizes his entire dependence on God, and therefore asks God to enter into the varied processes which govern his earthly life, both of heart and mind, of sight and speech, and into the final process of all – death.

The words require little explanation; but few as they are, they provide ample material for reflection and meditation.

God be in my head, and in my understanding. The head is the seat of the intelligence, the brain; and unquestionably the mind has an important place in the formulation of our faith. But here 'understanding' is more than mere knowledge, the kind of knowledge that can be acquired by book-learning. It is not simply an intellectual faculty. It includes the elements of spiritual insight and moral judgement.

If God is in our head, we shall have understanding of his ways with men and his purpose for the world; understanding too of the meaning of life, the value of people, and the significance of the created order.

As a result we shall see things in a new light. So we pray, *God be in my eyes, and in my looking*. The previous petition had to do with spiritual perception, with what St Paul called the eyes of the heart (Ephesians 1.18). This petition is concerned with natural sight, which is surely one of the most precious gifts we possess. And the vast majority of us do possess it, and we paid nothing for it, though in fact it is priceless.

What do we see with our eyes? One thing is certain. We have a different view of the world when God is in our looking. For the world is his, not ours. We did not make it: he did. Of the Eternal Word who became flesh, St John says, 'All things were made through him.' That fact not only enlarges our vision of Christ. It also enhances our appreciation of nature. In the words of the Victorian hymn writer, Godfrey Wade Robinson:

> Heaven above is softer blue,
> Earth around is sweeter green;
> Something lives in every hue
> Christless eyes have never seen;
> Birds with gladder songs o'erflow,
> Flowers with deeper beauties shine,
> Since I know, as now I know,
> I am his, and he is mine.

The third petition links what we see with what we say: *God be in my mouth, and in my speaking*. The Bible is a good deal concerned about our speaking, and this is scarcely surprising, for the words we utter are so powerful for good or evil. 'Death and life are in the power of the tongue' (Proverbs 18.21). What St James has to say about this is very much to the point (James 3.5–12). Jesus himself declared that by our words we shall be justified or condemned on the day of judgement (Matthew 12.36, 37). Wisely, then, we shall pray with the psalmist, 'Set a guard over my mouth, O Lord, and keep watch over the door of my lips' (Psalm 141.3).

It is out of the abundance of the *heart* that the mouth speaks, so we go on to pray, *God be in my heart, and in my thinking*. 'As a man thinketh in his heart, so is he.' The words of Proverbs 23.7 in the AV may not be an altogether accurate translation, but they express an undeniable truth. The thoughts of the heart represent the real person. They are a revelation of *character* – 'what a man is in the dark', as D. L. Moody put it.

Jesus said, 'The good man out of the good treasure of his heart produces good things' (Luke 6.45). The heart is the key to the matter. If God is in our hearts, we shall be free from evil desires and imaginations. Instead, we shall fill our thoughts with all that is true and noble, just and pure, lovely and gracious, all that is excellent and worthy of praise (Philippians 4.8).

If thus we think, thus also shall we live – and thus shall we die. So death when it comes need have no terrors, for we shall not face it alone: *God be at my end, and at my departing.*

My end will not be the end of everything. It will be the end only of this mortal existence, the dismantling of the earthly tent I now inhabit. In the best sense it will not be an end at all but a glorious new beginning, the taking possession of a building which God has provided: a house not made by human hands, eternal, and in heaven (2 Corinthians 5.1).

If God is at my end I shall have nothing to fear, and nothing to lose. Death will not be loss, but gain. My departing will be 'to depart and be with Christ, which is far better' (Philippians 1.23 AV). The word *depart* here has the meaning of 'to weigh anchor'. It is a picture word, rich in meaning. When we put out to sea on that final voyage we shall be homeward bound. So there need be 'no sadness of farewell' at our departing, as Tennyson expressed it:

> For though from out our bourne of Time and Place
> The flood may bear me far,
> I hope to see my Pilot face to face
> When I have crossed the bar.

Sir Francis Drake's Prayer

O Lord God, when thou givest to thy servants to endeavour any great matter, grant us also to know that it is not the beginning, but the continuing of the same unto the end, until it be thoroughly finished, which yieldeth the true glory; through him who for the finishing of thy work laid down his life, our Redeemer, Jesus Christ.

This prayer, which has become so widely known, was not written in this actual form by Sir Francis Drake (?1540–96). It was fashioned into a prayer (presumably by Dean Eric Milner-White) from a sentence Drake wrote, which is quoted after the prayer in *Daily Prayer*:

> There must be a begynning of any great matter, but the continewing unto the end untyll it be thoroughly finished yeldes the true glory.

The prayer expresses the thought as well as skilfully embodying the language of the great Elizabethan sailor. Drake would assuredly have approved of it, for he was himself a man of prayer. In a letter he wrote to John Foxe (author of the famous *Book of Martyrs*) from aboard his ship on the day he stormed Cadiz, he asked for continual remembrance in prayer, 'that our present service may take that good effect as God may be glorified, his Church, our Queen and country preserved, and the enemy of the truth utterly vanquished.'

In the sentence on which this prayer is based Drake insisted that there must be a *beginning* of any great matter; and the beginning is important. There are some who never get as far as that. They go no further than good intentions, well-meaning resolutions, brave talk. The temptation is one that besets us all. Wisely did Cardinal

Newman write: 'Fear not that your life should come to an end. Fear rather that it should never have a beginning.'

There must be a beginning; but as Drake discerned, *it is the continuing of the matter unto the end, until it be thoroughly finished, which yieldeth the true glory*. In the prayer we ask God to keep us mindful of this, so that we may be saved from beginning without finishing.

We may apply this to the 'great matter' of commitment to Christian discipleship. It is not difficult to become a Christian, or at any rate to make a profession of being one. It is much more difficult to keep it up and 'continue unto the end'. Many begin, but sooner or later fall away. Our country is littered with lapsed Christians – with people who, baptized and confirmed and one-time regular communicants, have failed to continue as they began.

Our Lord's parable of the Sower illustrates this. The seed sown on the shallow, rocky soil represents, he declared, 'those who receive the word with joy when they hear it, but have no root; they are believers for a while, but in the time of testing they desert' (Luke 8.13 NEB). No root – that is the real trouble; and the time of testing, when discipleship begins to cost, simply demonstrates what is lacking. Again and again one is reminded of G. K. Chesterton's dictum that Christianity has not been tried and found wanting, but tried and found too hard.

Drake's words apply equally to the service we undertake in the life of the Church. We are ready enough, it may be, to embark upon some work for God, whether or not it be a great matter. But all too easily we get discouraged or lose interest and give up before the task is thoroughly finished. In the words of Jesus, we put our hand to the plough but look back (Luke 9.62). We lack the grace (or is it the grit?) to persevere. Service of that kind, as Drake discerned, does not yield the true glory.

St Paul, recalling his life of service for Christ, could say at the end of his days, 'I have finished the course', or as a modern translation puts it, 'I have run the full distance' (2 Timothy 4.7 GNB). For him the race was over – but it was completed.

The words added at the end of the prayer form a particularly fitting conclusion: *through him who for the finishing of thy work laid down his life, our Redeemer, Jesus Christ*. He, for the joy that was set before him, endured the cross and despised its shame, till at last he could cry in triumph, 'It is finished!' Jesus is our great exemplar as well as our Redeemer; and as the writer to the Hebrews says, we are to keep our eyes fixed on him (12.2). He who endures to the end shall be saved.

Sir Walter Raleigh's Prayer

Give me my scallop-shell of quiet;
My staff of faith to walk upon;
My scrip of joy, immortal diet;
My bottle of salvation;
My gown of glory (hope's true gage);
And thus I'll take my pilgrimage.

Sir Walter Raleigh (1552–1618) was one of the most colourful characters of the Elizabethan age. Soldier, courtier, adventurer, poet, he was a man of many parts and led a life of strangely mixed fortunes. At the height of his career he enjoyed the favour of his Queen and was loaded with wealth and honours; but in his later years he fell victim to the intrigues of his enemies, who successfully accused him of conspiring against James I and he was condemned to death. At his execution, when he was asked which way he preferred to lay his head on the block, he replied, 'So long as the heart be right, it matters not which way the head lies.'

This prayer of his (from 'The Passionate Man's Pilgrimage') would seem to indicate that his heart was right. More than sixty years before Bunyan wrote his *Pilgrim's Progress*, Raleigh portrayed the Christian life in the same allegorical terms. His is a pilgrim's prayer. The last line provides the key: 'And thus I'll take my pilgrimage.' *Thus* – that is, with the things he has asked for as he prepares for life's journey. Those things are designated in the language of poetry.

First, *Give me my scallop-shell of quiet.* The significance of those words is likely to elude us unless we understand that in medieval times the scallop-shell was the recognized emblem of a pilgrim. So this pilgrim is duly wearing his badge. But that is not all. Raleigh pictures his scallop-shell serving as a small receptacle, filled with quiet. He wants to pursue his pilgrimage with a peaceful heart. Whatever the perils, hardships, conflicts and adventures to be encountered on the way, he craves for inner tranquility, for a quiet mind.

And next: *My staff of faith to walk upon.* The staff was part of the pilgrim's equipment. It was not simply his defence in time of danger. More still, it afforded him support along the pilgrim way. It gave him something to lean upon. We too need something to lean upon in our pilgrimage; and this is where faith comes in, for we walk by faith, not by sight. So we may say, in the words of the hymn by Thomas Lynch (1818–71):

> My faith is as an oaken staff,
> The traveller's well-loved aid.

My scrip of joy, immortal diet. The scrip represents another piece of the pilgrim's equipment. It was a small bag or pack in which he carried his provisions (*cf.* Matthew 10.10). But why here his 'scrip of joy'? And how is this 'immortal diet'? The reference seems to be to joy of a divine quality, the 'joy unspeakable and full of glory' (1 Peter 1.8 AV). This heavenly joy nourishes and fortifies us on our journey. The joy of the Lord is our strength. Or to put it in other biblical words, the Lord is both our strength and our song.

The pilgrim carries not only a scrip for food but a bottle for drink – *My bottle of salvation.* The psalmist uses a somewhat similar metaphor when he says, 'I will take in my hands the cup of salvation and invoke the name of the Lord' (116.13). The cup of salvation is filled from the bottle of salvation; and to carry the metaphor a stage further, we may say that in our journey we draw water from the wells of salvation with which to replenish our bottle (Isaiah 12.3). To put it simply, God's saving grace is always available, always sufficient:

> Grace, which like the Lord the giver,
> Never fails from age to age.

Salvation has a future tense; hence the final petition for *My gown of glory (hope's true gage).* The two keywords here are 'glory' and 'hope'. They are two of the great New Testament words which speak of the eternal future, the life to come. St Paul brings them together when he says, 'We rejoice in the hope of the glory of God'

(Romans 5.2). That surpassing glory is the goal of our pilgrimage; and our Christian hope pledges that it shall be ours at last when this mortal nature will be clothed with immortality (1 Corinthians 15.53).

Robert Louis Stevenson declared that it is better to travel hopefully than to arrive. There is wisdom in that, of course; but it is better still to travel hopefully *and* to arrive. And that is what the Christian pilgrim may look forward to with confidence. With a quiet spirit, a firm faith, a heavenly joy, the means of grace and the hope of glory, he can say, *And thus I'll take my pilgrimage.*

A Prayer after John Donne

Bring us, O Lord God, at our last awakening into the house and gate of heaven, to enter into that gate and dwell in that house, where there shall be no darkness nor dazzling, but one equal light; no noise nor silence, but one equal music; no fears nor hopes, but one equal possession; no ends nor beginnings, but one equal eternity; in the habitations of thy glory and dominion world without end.

John Donne (1573–1631) was one of the leading poets and preachers of the seventeenth century. He was deeply influenced by his early religious training as a member of a Roman Catholic family, but while in his twenties he embraced the faith of the Church of England. It was not until he reached the age of forty-two that, largely under pressure from the King, he was ordained and became a royal chaplain. Six years later (1621) he was appointed Dean of St Paul's, where his sermons attracted large congregations. His poetry, though of the 'metaphysical' school and not always easy to understand, also won him considerable fame.

This prayer on the Life Everlasting is derived from one of his sermons. The question is often asked, What is heaven like? In the prayer Donne answers it in the language of poetry, the sort of metaphysical poetry to which we have referred. No human language can describe the future life, for it lies totally outside our present experience. We can conceive of it only by means of metaphors and images drawn from life as it now is. This is what we find in the Bible (e.g. in the book of Revelation) and similarly here in John Donne's prayer.

The prayer starts by referring to the end of this life as *our last awakening* – that is, our awakening from the sleep of death in the life beyond; and we pray that God will then *bring us to the house and gate of heaven*, so that by entering that gate we may dwell in that house. Jesus spoke of heaven as 'my Father's house' (John 14.2). Donne adopts this symbol and gives it a poetical description in the four clauses which make up the body of the prayer.

The clauses all follow the same general pattern. They depict the perfection of heaven by contrasting certain extremes (as, e.g., darkness and light in the first clause) and employing the word *equal* in the sense of evenly proportioned, perfectly balanced.

First, then, in the heavenly house *there shall be no darkness nor dazzling, but one equal light*. Darkness is the absence of light; dazzling is an excess of light. The light of heaven is neither of these but light in its perfection. 'The (heavenly) city has no need of sun or moon to shine upon it, for the glory of God is its light, and its lamp is the Lamb' (Revelation 21.23).

From the simile of sight the prayer turns to that of sound: *no noise nor silence, but one equal music*. Noise in the form of clangour, din, cacophony is a horrible thing, destructive of all peace. Such noise has no place in the music of heaven. Nor has a terrifying, isolating silence, devoid of speech or song. There will be one equal music, melody in perfection, transcendentally lovely. The Book of Revelation gives us a foretaste of heaven's music: the sound of harpers playing on their harps (14.2), myriads of angels praising the Lamb who was slain (5.11, 12), and the voice of a great multitude singing a Hallelujah chorus (19.1–6).

Again, in the house of heaven there shall be *no fears nor hopes, but one equal possession*. Fears represent the things we dread, hopes the things we desire. We shall have no fears in heaven, for what we feared will then have ceased to exist. Likewise we shall have no hopes in heaven, for what we hoped for will then be ours – one equal possession. The word which best interprets this clause of the prayer is *fulfilment*. Much of our life in this world remains unfulfilled, unsatisfied, incomplete. Heaven will mean the possession of all we have lacked, or needed, or longed for.

And in heaven there will be *no ends nor beginnings, but one equal eternity*. Here we meet with the element of time. Our life in this world is governed by the time factor, by clocks and calendars, by hours and days, months and years, with their beginnings and ends. But the life beyond is timeless. It has 'no ends nor beginnings'. Heaven is where God is, and is eternal like himself. Likewise all that pertains to it shares the quality of infinitude. In contemplating such an order of existence we creatures of time are hopelessly out of our depth. It is beyond our comprehension; but by God's rich mercy in Christ it is not beyond our attainment.

What is heaven like? John Donne supplies part of the answer to the question in somewhat abstruse and mystical terms. Probably for most of us it is sufficient to know that heaven is the Father's house, with its 'many mansions' or rooms – *the habitations of his glory and dominion world without end.*

Sir Jacob Astley's Prayer

O Lord, thou knowest how busy I must be this day. If I forget thee, do not thou forget me.

The prayer is said to have been used by Sir Jacob Astley before the Battle of Edgehill on 23 October 1642 – the first battle of the Civil War between the armies of Charles I and the Earl of Essex.

If the tradition is true, we can understand Sir Jacob's sentiments when he prayed, *O Lord, thou knowest how busy I must be this day*. It was the prayer of a busy man, and it is therefore a prayer for busy people. And most of us are busy people, or think we are. Indeed, in a world in which so much waits to be done, we all ought to be busy. To be busy is better than to be idle.

Yet busyness itself is not a virtue. It can become a fault. It is possible to be over busy, to have too many irons in the fire. It is possible to do a lot and achieve very little. William Cowper speaks somewhere of 'the busy trifler'. To be busy and yet to trifle is indeed a sorry business. Perhaps some of us would achieve more if we were to do less.

This is certainly true in the Christian life. The story of Martha and Mary in St Luke's Gospel has something to say to us here (10.38–42). Martha was entertaining Jesus in their Bethany home, and as she prepared the meal she 'was distracted with much serving'. Mary, on the other hand, sat at the Lord's feet and listened to his teaching.

The story significantly follows immediately upon the parable of the Good Samaritan with its emphasis on service. 'Go and do likewise,' Jesus says at the end. It would seem that Martha was obeying that injunction as she busied herself in the kitchen. Yet the Lord rebuked her: not so much for what she *was* doing but for what she was failing to do – for neglecting the 'better part' which Mary had chosen, that of hearing the word of God. As E. Earle Ellis comments, 'The issue is not two kinds of Christian service but religious busyness which distracts the Christian – preacher or layman – from the word of Christ upon which all effective service rests.'[1]

To be busy is good, but something else matters more. It was a saying of Bishop J. Taylor Smith: 'Beware of the barrenness of a busy life.' To that we may add another saying: if you are too busy to pray, you are too busy.

If I forget thee, do not thou forget me. Sir Jacob could be sure, in actual fact, that in the busy day ahead the Lord would not forget him. And we can share the same certainty. God's steadfast, enduring love ensures that we are never forgotten by him. When ancient Zion lamented: 'The Lord has forsaken me, my God has forgotten me,' God's answer through the prophet was: 'Can a woman forget the infant at her breast, or a loving mother the child in her womb? Even these forget, yet I will not forget you' (Isaiah 49.14, 15 NEB). A mother's love for her child is strong indeed, but it is not perfect. God's love for his people is stronger still, invincible, unchanging, eternal.

God will not forget us. But what if we forget him in the midst of our busy lives, with so many things claiming our attention? Perhaps the simple answer to that question is that the loss is ours. The more busy we are, the more we need to remember God and call upon his help as we go about our work. It is possible to be both busy and prayerful at the same time.

Nehemiah provides us with a good illustration. He was the royal cupbearer, and was kept busy fulfilling his duties; but as he waited on the king he did not forget God. In a moment of crisis he sent up a swift 'arrow prayer' to heaven, and his prayer was as swiftly answered (Nehemiah 2.4; see also 6.9, 13, 14, 22).

Or we may think of Brother Lawrence, the seventeenth century lay monk in the Carmelite monastery in Paris where he was given charge of the kitchen. The work was humdrum, and he was kept endlessly busy; but as he went about his duties he constantly recollected God and lifted up his heart to him. His prayer in fact was the practice of the presence of God. So he wrote: 'We should establish ourselves in the sense of God's presence by continually conversing with him.'

Alongside Sir Jacob Astley's prayer we might place a prayer by Bishop W. Walsham How (1823–97):

> O heavenly Father, in whom we live and move and have our being, we humbly pray thee so to guide and govern us by thy Holy Spirit, that in all the cares and occupations of our daily life we may never forget thee, but remember that we are ever walking in thy sight.

And there is another suitable prayer for busy people, said to have been written by a medieval monk:

> Lord, temper with tranquillity
> Our manifold activity,
> That we may do our work for thee
> With very great simplicity.

Note

[1] *The Gospel of Luke* (Oliphants, 1973), p. 160.

Cardinal Newman's Prayer

O Lord, support us all the day long of this troublous life, until the shades lengthen, and the evening comes, and the busy world is hushed, the fever of life is over, and our work is done. Then, Lord, in thy mercy, grant us safe lodging, a holy rest, and peace at the last; through Jesus Christ our Lord.

The source of the words which make up this prayer is a passage at the end of a sermon by John Henry Newman (1801–90) beginning, 'Let us beg of him (our Lord) to stand by us in trouble . . .' A sentence or two later come the words:

> May he support us all the day long, till the shades lengthen, and the evening comes, and the busy world is hushed, and the fever of life is over, and our work done. Then in his mercy may he give us a safe lodging, and holy rest, and peace at the last!

It has been suggested that in using these words Newman was quoting from some earlier (possibly sixteenth century) writer; but there is no suggestion of this in the sermon, and if the words are a quotation it is strange, to say the least, that their author has never been identified after all this time. It is entirely reasonable to conclude that the words are Cardinal Newman's own. Some unknown editor refashioned them into a prayer, and ever since the prayer was included among the Occasional Prayers in the 1928 Prayer Book it has become very well known.

The prayer has something in common with Lyte's hymn 'Abide with me', based on the prayer of the disciples at Emmaus. When he wrote the hymn Lyte was a dying man, and he knew it. He was conscious that for him 'life's little day' was swiftly drawing to its close, and his prayer was that he might know the presence of the living Christ as the shadows gathered round him in the evening of life.

Newman's prayer points in the same direction; but it begins by asking for the Lord's *support*, not only at the evening hour but *all the day long* – that is, throughout the whole course of life, from start to finish. For it is a *troublous life*, seldom wholly free from trials and adversities. 'Man is born to trouble as the sparks fly upward,' said Eliphaz to Job, and he was doubtless right (Job 5.7). Every stage of our earthly journey has its peculiar perils and temptations. Therefore all our life long we need to be supported by the Everlasting Arms and to pray, 'Hold up my goings in thy path, that my footsteps slip not' (Psalm 17.5 AV).

We do not know when for us life's day will end, but our prayer is that the Lord will support us *until the shades lengthen, and the evening comes*. Here we are back with Lyte again: 'fast falls the eventide'. It is life's sunset hour. The shadows grow longer in the fading light of day. *The busy world is hushed*, for now we are detached from its restless and ceaseless activity. *The fever of life is over*. Nothing more remains to be accomplished: *our work is done*.

Such is Newman's poetic description of life's final phase. It makes an immediate appeal to the imagination; but we must candidly recognize that it is not only a poetic but also an idyllic description. Death, as we know, does not always come in so gentle and kindly a fashion. It may be violent, abrupt, painful. The light of earthly day may not gradually fade but be suddenly extinguished. We must face this fact and pray, in the words of the Litany, that the good Lord may deliver us from 'sudden (i.e. unprepared) death'.

And after death? *Then, Lord, in thy mercy, grant us safe lodging, a holy rest, and peace at the last*. We may not be sure what exact meaning Newman attached to these words. He was a Roman Catholic. I am writing as an Anglican. Yet I do not forget that Newman himself had been an Anglican until the age of forty-four, and maybe his interpretation would not have been all that different from mine.

At any rate, on one fundamental point we would be agreed. Whatever we hope for after death is altogether of God's *mercy*. We have no merits of our own to plead. We are as much debtors to mercy in the life to come as in this present life.

'Safe lodging' is what we ask for first. And what safer lodging can there be than what Jesus called the Father's house (John 14.2)? We pass our time here on earth in a state of insecurity, for our present lodging is a frail human body, no more than a temporary abode. St Paul likens it to a tent which will one day be dismantled and exchanged for 'a house not made with hands, eternal in the heavens' (2 Corinthians 5.1). The Father's house provides a safe, secure lodging. In Professor R. V. G. Tasker's words, 'It is a permanent home, from which eviction is impossible, and where no notice to quit can ever be served!'

Again, we pray that 'a holy rest' may be ours when we are released from the turmoils and struggles of this world. Richard Baxter, the seventeenth century Puritan divine, wrote a devotional classic entitled *The Saints' Everlasting Rest* (1650). What an alluring prospect for those whose life on earth has been a long, hard, incessant grind! 'Blessed are the dead who die in the Lord,' we are told, 'for they shall rest from their labours' (Revelation 14.13). But while their toil is over, we may be sure that their service continues. The rest that remains for the people of God (Hebrews 4.9) is far from being a sort of armchair existence. 'It is not the end of activity but the end of futile striving, in uninterrupted fellowship with God' (William Neil).

'And peace at the last,' is our final plea. The peace we seek, I take it, is the peace of God's presence. If we ask, What is heaven? Where is heaven? the short answer is that heaven is where God is and where God reigns. 'Behold, a throne was set in heaven,' says the seer of the Apocalypse, 'and One sat on the throne!' The throne (mentioned over thirty times in the Apocalypse) is the symbol of God's sovereignty. His rule of perfect love abolishes all the disharmony created by man's sin and rebellion. At the last, then, we shall enter into God's peace. Best of all, we shall dwell with the God of peace, safe and at rest for ever beneath the shadow of his throne.

The Master Carpenter Prayer

Jesus, Master Carpenter of Nazareth, who on the cross through wood and nails didst work man's whole salvation: Wield well thy tools in this thy workshop; that we who come to thee rough hewn may by thy hand be fashioned to a truer beauty and a greater usefulness, for the honour of thy name.

'Is not this the carpenter, the son of Mary?' was the question asked by the people of Nazareth when Jesus returned to his home town (Mark 6.3). During those hidden years, as he grew into manhood, Jesus had worked at the bench and earned his living as the village carpenter. It was thus that his own people remembered him. It is an arresting picture.

> Behold the Son of God in His lowly humility! A workman at His trade, a carpenter earning money . . . And so He taught mankind for ever the dignity of honest labour in the sight of God. Think how Jesus the artisan has ennobled all honest work. The carpenter at his bench can feel comradeship with his Lord.[1]

The prayer adopts this concept of Jesus as the *Master Carpenter of Nazareth* and spiritualizes it. The prayer dates back to the first World War, having been written, as far as is known, by Hal Pink of Toc H. It appears in different books in slightly varying forms but always employing the same striking imagery. The version used here is reproduced from my *Parish Prayers*.

As a carpenter Jesus worked with wood and nails, and this fact calls to mind the death he was to die – the death of the cross. It was *through wood and nails* that at the last he wrought *man's whole salvation*. The ghastly instrument of death and shame became in God's loving wisdom the emblem of life and glory.

This thought lifts the prayer at the outset to a high spiritual level. The humble village carpenter was destined to be the world's redeemer. His death, crowned by his resurrection, was his greatest work, his finest achievement. 'He himself bore our sins in his body on the tree,' wrote the apostle Peter (1 Peter 2.24); and in using the word 'tree' he was referring to the *wood* of the cross, as the Greek word indicates. The wood to which the Son of God was nailed at Calvary was the same material he had once handled day by day at the carpenter's bench.

Our petition now follows. *Wield well thy tools in this thy workshop* – the workshop of the world in which there are so many damaged and broken lives, our own included; *that we who come to thee rough hewn may by thy hand be fashioned to a truer beauty and a greater usefulness.*

The language carries us back again to Nazareth where the young carpenter, the son of Mary, skilfully employs his hands and tools in the making and mending of things. But at this point there is a change in our own position in relation to the prayer. So far we have been observers, watching the carpenter at work as he carries out his various tasks. Now, however, we ourselves are involved in what he is doing. We bring our own lives to him as rough and ready material and ask him to do with us, and make of us, what he will. We know well enough that there are things in our characters that need to be changed if we are to become the sort of people he wants us to be, 'consecrated and useful to the Master . . . ready for any good work' (2 Timothy 2.21).

The transforming power of Christ in human life is illustrated throughout the New Testament. Nowhere is it more strikingly revealed than in the lives of the men he chose at the very beginning to form the company of the Twelve. They came to him rough hewn, but in his hands they were fashioned into something altogether finer, fit instruments for his service. Thus Simon Peter, that impetuous, unstable character, became the man of rock. John, the son of thunder, was changed into the apostle of love. Thomas, the man who was 'doubtful in thy Son's resurrection', as the collect puts it, became a bold confessor of the faith.

The Master Carpenter can do something of the same with us if we too place ourselves in his hands and let him have his way with us. Of course, it won't happen all at once. The reshaping of human lives is a slow process, and sometimes a painful one. The Carpenter's tools may cut. But in his hands they are safe, and we can trust him implicitly. As Newman wrote, 'He does nothing in vain. He knows what he is about.'

Note

[1]J. Paterson Smythe, *A People's Life of Christ* (Hodder & Stoughton, 1921), pp. 69, 70.

Reinhold Niebuhr's Prayer

God grant me the serenity
to accept the things I cannot change,
the courage to change the things I can,
and the wisdom to know the difference.

This prayer by Reinhold Niebuhr (1892–1971), the distinguished American theologian, has gained a good deal of popularity. It is not difficult to see why. As a scholar, Niebuhr's aim was to relate theology to life and society, and in a sense this is what the prayer does. It has a plain, practical, down-to-earth quality.

It is a prayer about *acceptance*: about the things in life we should accept and those we should not. And corresponding to this it is a prayer about *change*: about the things we cannot change and those we can – and should.

It begins by recognizing quite honestly that there are things in life which we *cannot change* and which therefore we must be prepared to *accept*. And our prayer is that we may accept them, not with stoical resignation or with a sense of grievance, but with *serenity*. The word is well chosen. It comes from the Latin *serenus*, meaning clear, bright, unclouded. So here what we are asking God to give us is a calm, unruffled faith, undisturbed by life's inevitable ills and adversities: a faith which bravely faces facts and is not an escape from reality and which therefore accepts what cannot be changed. The alternative to such acceptance is resentment, leading to bitterness of spirit.

Of the things we cannot change the most obvious example is death. Someone very dear to us dies. It is something that is happening every day. Even so, when it happens to us we may find it a most difficult thing to accept. And doubtless the greater our love, the harder the acceptance. Yet the thing has happened, and we have to come to terms with the finality of death – as far as this world is concerned. But only as far as this world is concerned. It is here that faith enters the scene. As believers we can accept death with serenity, because we know that death is not the end and that the separation it brings is not for ever. We do not grieve over those who have 'fallen asleep' as men who have no hope (1 Thessalonians 4.13).

Another unchangeable thing we may be called upon to accept is an incurable disease or bodily handicap, such as blindness. St Paul's 'thorn in the flesh' provides a good biblical illustration (2 Corinthians 12.7–10). The exact nature of his affliction is not known. All sorts of guesses have been made; but one thing is clear: the apostle's suffering was of a physical nature. His 'thorn' was in the *flesh*. Epilepsy, malarial fever, or ophthalmia are the most likely suggestions offered. Three times he prayed that the infirmity might be healed or removed; but the Lord's answer was, 'My grace is sufficient for you, for my power is made perfect in weakness.' The outcome was that Paul learned to accept his affliction with a serene faith, in total reliance upon the grace of God.

Along with the things we cannot alter but only accept are the things we *can change* – and we ask for *courage* to do so. In such a situation we may be tempted to acquiesce and do nothing; and that requires not courage but simply complacency. It is easy enough to adopt a sort of fatalistic attitude to the evils of the world. After all, these things have always existed. They are part of the structure of our human society. They are too deep-rooted to be changed. And in any case it is somebody else's business, not ours.

Courage is what we need. Without that heroic quality, the dedicated men and women who have rid the world of some of its worst abuses and transformed the face of society would never have succeeded. Think of the courage required of people like William Wilberforce, Elizabeth Fry, John Howard, Lord Shaftesbury, Josephine Butler, William Booth and a host of other reformers. The tasks they tackled were gigantic. The odds against them were enormous. But they refused to give up. They had the courage to fight, to persevere and to win.

Something of that same courage we pray may be given to us as we in our own day face things that cry out to be changed. At the root of all that needs changing is man's fallen nature. And you can't change that, it is often asserted. True enough: *you* can't change it. But God can. If the gospel of his grace means anything at all, it is the good news that the heart of man can undergo a radical transformation and he can become a 'new creation' in Christ.

To accept the things that cannot be changed requires serenity, and to change the things that can be changed requires courage; but how are we *to know the difference* between the two situations? We may not find it easy to decide; and that is why we ask for a third quality: *wisdom*. God-given serenity and God-given courage are not sufficient without God-given wisdom.

Without that discernment we may become fretful in face of things that cannot be changed and forfeit a peace that should be ours. On the other hand, we may become complacent when challenged by things that can be changed, and be lulled into a peace that should not be ours. The wisdom to know the difference is what St James calls 'the wisdom from above', for it is a heavenly, not a human faculty. And he encourages us to pray for it when he writes: 'If any of you falls short in wisdom, he should ask God for it and it will be given him, for God is a generous giver who neither refuses nor reproaches anyone' (James 3.17; 1.5 NEB).

Two

THE BOOK OF COMMON PRAYER

Introduction

The prayers dealt with in this section are derived from different periods. Some belong to the Reformation era and were composed for one or other of the versions of the Prayer Book which appeared between 1549 and 1662. Others are translations of Latin collects from the ancient Sacramentaries, the liturgical books which contained the order of the Communion or Mass and the variable prayers for use throughout the year. In the Western Church three such books were widely influential: the Leonine Sacramentary, dating from the early seventh century; the Gelasian, late seventh century; and the Gregorian, eighth century. The famous Popes after whom they are named were all of earlier date and their connection with the Sacramentaries is largely conjectural.

Among the books I have consulted are the *Prayer Book Dictionary* and Evan Daniel's well known handbook and commentary; *The Book of English Collects*, edited by J. W. Suter, Jr. (Harper, 1940); J. H. B. Masterman's *Sunday Collects* (SPCK, 1916); and L. E. H. Stephens-Hodge's book on *The Collects* in the Prayer Book Commentaries (Hodder & Stoughton, 1961).

The Collect for Grace

O Lord, our heavenly Father, Almighty and everlasting God, who hast safely brought us to the beginning of this day: Defend us in the same with thy mighty power; and grant that this day we fall into no sin, neither run into any kind of danger; but that all our doings may be ordered by thy governance, to do always that is righteous in thy sight; through Jesus Christ our Lord.

The service of Morning Prayer is made up of material drawn from the monastic offices (or Hour Services) of Mattins, Lauds, and Prime in the Sarum Breviary. The Breviary was the book which contained these daily services. Thus the Venite and Te Deum came from Mattins (before daybreak); the Benedicite and the Collect for Peace from Lauds (at daybreak); and the Apostles' Creed, the Lord's Prayer, and the present collect from Prime (at about 6 a.m.). Cranmer skilfully combined these and other elements to make up a new service for morning worship.

The Collect for Grace, as it is called in the BCP, came at the end of Prime. It is derived from the Gelasian Sacramentary and so has been in use in the Church for nearly fourteen centuries.

The opening words are particularly impressive: *O Lord, our heavenly Father, Almighty and everlasting God*. At first sight the two sentences might appear to be merely repetitive. One or other of these invocations would surely be sufficient. Yet a closer look reveals that they are not identical but are rather complementary. He whom we approach with joy and confidence as our heavenly Father is also the Almighty and everlasting God before whom we bow in reverence and awe. There is a reminder here that freedom in prayer must never give place to flippancy. 'Our Father' is also our

Father 'in heaven' – that is, transcendent in glory, majesty, and power.

The words *who hast safely brought us to the beginning of this day* are by implication a thanksgiving. Perhaps they should be made explicitly so, as in the amended version of the collect: 'we thank you that you have brought us safely to the beginning of this day' (ASB). In the words of the psalmist: 'It is good to give thanks to the Lord . . . to declare thy steadfast love in the morning' (92.1).

The reference to the 'beginning' of the day is explained by the collect's origin in the early morning office of Prime. When, as is often the case, Mattins is said later in the morning, the word loses something of its significance. Nevertheless the fact remains that each new day is a fresh gift from God, to be received in a spirit of gratitude for his safe keeping of us during the night.

How are we to face the new day that lies ahead? With a sense of our own frailty and in dependence on God's grace: *Defend us in the same with thy mighty power; and grant that this day we fall into no sin, neither run into any kind of danger*. It is reassuring to know that God's almighty power is our defence and that our lives are in his strong hands; and in that confidence we pray that in the day before us we may 'fall into no sin' – which is really what we mean when in the Lord's Prayer we say, 'Lead us not into temptation.' Thus we recognize the spiritual perils that beset us in our daily lives, and pray to be kept from sinning.

But there are perils of another kind to be encountered, which is why we also ask that we may not 'run into any kind of danger'. The reference here would seem to be to physical harm, to accident, injury, and illness. In the words of the ancient office hymn for Prime (as translated by J. M. Neale):

> Now that the daylight fills the sky,
> We lift our hearts to God on high,
> That he, in all we do or say,
> Would keep us free from harm today.

The last part of the collect takes on a more positive character. Our prayer now is not only that we may be guarded from sin and danger, *but that all our doings may be ordered by thy governance, to do always that is righteous in thy sight*.

The American Prayer Book gives a better grammatical construction to these closing words by rendering them: 'but that all our doings, being ordered by thy governance, may be righteous in thy sight'. In the ASB the words are: 'order us in all our doings and guide us to do always what is right in your eyes.'

However we render the prayer, it is a request that God may so rule our lives that all our actions may be in conformity to his will and be right in his sight. What God sees in us and thinks about our lives matters more than the world's judgement. Our aim should be, in Milton's well known words, to live as ever in our great Task-Master's eye.

Even so, we do well to remember that it was St Paul's concern to have a conscience void of offence towards both God and men (Acts 24.16); and he urged God's people to 'aim at what is honourable not only in the Lord's sight but also in the sight of men' (2 Corinthians 8.21).

Vesper Collect

Lighten our darkness, we beseech thee, O Lord; and by thy great mercy defend us from all perils and dangers of this night; for the love of thy only Son, our Saviour Jesus Christ.

In the Sarum Breviary this Gelasian collect was part of the office of Vespers. In putting together the Prayer Book service of Evensong, Cranmer drew upon material from both Vespers (the evening office) and Compline (the service before retiring to rest). From Vespers came also the Magnificat, while the Nunc Dimittis was derived from Compline.

In the BCP this Vesper collect is called 'The Third Collect, for Aid against all Perils'. The perils are referred to more particularly in the second part of the prayer. It begins with the words *Lighten our darkness, we beseech thee, O Lord*. How are we to understand this? What are we asking for when we ask God to 'lighten our darkness'?

Various interpretations have been offered. For example, it has been suggested that here we are praying that our minds may be enlightened to know God's unsleeping care. The revised version of the prayer in the new American Prayer Book begins 'Be light in our darkness, O Lord.' This is probably the meaning most people attach to the words. They are asking for spiritual illumination amid the darkness of the night.

Such, of course, is a perfectly proper prayer, and no exception can be taken to it; but it is doubtful whether this is what the collect is really saying. 'Lighten our darkness' is a concise and compressed way of asking God to bring us through the darkness of the night to the light of a new day. And the remainder of the prayer is a request that throughout the night, till daylight breaks, the Lord will watch over us and defend us from harm.

There is no occasion to spiritualize the opening words and give them a symbolical meaning. Both light and darkness are perfectly natural entities and are simply other terms for day and night. As the day ends and the night enfolds us we pray that we may be spared to see the light of another day.

The hours of darkness are not without their hazards, and so we go on to pray: *and of thy great mercy defend us from all perils and dangers of this night.* As in the corresponding morning collect, dealt with in the previous study, we ask God to 'defend us'. We need his protection by night as well as by day. The 'perils and dangers' of the night are real and not imaginary.

A little reflection will soon convince us that this is so. Thieves operate at night. Fires break out in the night. Illness may strike by night. Storm and wind, lightning and tempest, are also among the perils of the night, to say nothing of the perils which, all unknown to us, providentially pass us by.

There are dangers or evils of another kind which we ought not to forget. We are reminded of them in the ancient Compline hymn when we pray:

> From all ill dreams defend our eyes,
> From nightly fears and fantasies;
> Tread under foot our ghostly foe,
> That no pollution we may know.

And what of the day's cares and anxieties which we take to bed with us and brood over wakefully in the long watches of the night? From sleeplessness too we need God to defend us.

Day and night is the recurring pattern of our lives. The psalmist found comfort in the fact that with God day and night are both alike. 'The darkness is not dark to thee, the night is bright as the day; for darkness is as light with thee' (Psalm 139.12). This may also be our comfort and confidence at the ending of the day.

Bishop Heber's stanza sums up our reflections on the Vesper collect:

> God, that madest earth and heaven,
> Darkness and light;
> Who the day for toil hast given,
> For rest the night;

May thine angel-guards defend us,
Slumber sweet thy mercy send us,
Holy dreams and hopes attend us,
This livelong night.

A Prayer of Saint Chrysostom

Almighty God, who hast given us grace at this time with one accord to make our common supplications unto thee; and dost promise that when two or three are gathered together in thy Name thou wilt grant their requests: Fulfil now, O Lord, the desires and petitions of thy servants, as may be most expedient for them; granting us in this world knowledge of thy truth, and in the world to come life everlasting.

The title of this prayer in the BCP is misleading. Although it is ascribed to St John Chrysostom (344–407), the famous Patriarch of Constantinople, its actual authorship is not known. It seems that Cranmer took the prayer from the so-called Liturgy of St Chrysostom and named the prayer accordingly; but the liturgy is of much later date than Chrysostom himself and has little if any direct connection with him. A Latin edition of the Greek text had been published in 1528 and Cranmer probably used this as the basis of his English translation. He included the prayer at the end of the Litany he wrote in 1544, and five years later this became part of the first English Prayer Book. The prayer was not added to the services of Morning and Evening Prayer until 1662.

It is important to note that the prayer is addressed to God the Son, as is clear from the language as a whole. The opening words *Almighty God* are a later addition and give the impression that the prayer is addressed to the Father. A different opening is really required, or an adjustment should be made in the later wording, as in the American Prayer Book of 1977 ('you have promised through your well-beloved Son that when two or three are gathered together in his Name . . .'). The ASB gives the prayer in two forms: first as in the BCP, with the personal pronouns changed, and secondly in a completely new and much altered version. This latter is not altogether satisfactory, and among other things it omits the reference to the 'two or three' gathered to pray.

Clearly the prayer is designed to be said at the end of prayers, hence its appropriate place both in the Litany and in the daily offices. With a sense of gratitude we acknowledge that the Lord has *given us grace at this time with one accord to make our common supplications*. Prayer is all a matter of grace. It is by God's grace that we are permitted to pray to him. It is his grace which enables us to pray. And it is of his grace that he answers our prayers. So prayer is not only a means of grace. It is also a mark of God's grace or favour towards us.

The reference here is to corporate, not private, prayer. We are making our 'common supplications', the prayers which we have in common. We therefore offer them 'with one accord', in unity of spirit, with one heart and mind. This has a bearing on what follows in the next part of the prayer: our Lord's *promise that when two or three are gathered together in (his) Name* he will *grant their requests*. The promise in question is this (Matthew 18.19, 20 AV):

> If two of you shall agree on earth as touching anything that they shall ask, it shall be done for them of my Father which is in heaven. For where two or three are gathered together in my name, there am I in the midst of them.

In these words the Lord gives a twofold assurance to his disciples when two or three of them meet in his name and agree about what they ask. First, God will answer their prayer; and second, he himself will be spiritually present in their midst.

The prayer we are looking at combines these lines of thought. It may be only the two or three who gather to pray, but because they do so in harmony of purpose and meet in the name of Jesus, God will *grant their requests*.

In this confidence we make our petition: *Fulfil now, O Lord, the desires and petitions of thy servants, as may be most expedient for them*. The 'desires' are the unspoken longings of our hearts; the 'petitions' are the prayers we have expressed in words. God who hears our petitions also knows our desires; so we ask that he will fulfil both alike, 'as may be most expedient for us'.

The qualification we make in those last words is a wise one. We do not always realise what is most expedient for us. In our ignorance we may well pray for what is inexpedient and not in our best interests. The psalmist says of the Israelites that the Lord 'gave them their request, but sent leanness into their soul' (Psalm 106.15 AV). We must recognize that God in his love and wisdom knows what is for our ultimate good and ask him to determine the issue of our prayers accordingly.

Finally, we make another request. We pray that the Lord will grant us *in this world knowledge of (his) truth, and in the world to come life everlasting*. The two clauses are closely related. 'The knowledge of saving truth in this world is the first step to life everlasting in the world to come' (Evan Daniel). And let us not forget that Christ himself is the embodiment of the truth and the life, and the way to both. To possess him is to possess everything, here and hereafter.

The Collect for Purity

Almighty God, unto whom all hearts be open, all desires known, and from whom no secrets are hid: Cleanse the thoughts of our hearts by the inspiration of thy Holy Spirit, that we may perfectly love thee, and worthily magnify thy holy Name; through Christ our Lord.

Few prayers are more familiar to Anglican worshippers than the Collect for Purity, as it is known. Dating back in its original Latin form to the sixth century, it was used in the Sarum Missal (the order of Mass) as part of the priest's private preparation before the service. Cranmer incorporated it into the actual liturgy in the first English Prayer Book (1549), and there it has retained its place ever since. Nowadays the collect is said not by the celebrant alone but by the whole congregation, as a corporate act of preparation for the Holy Communion.

There could scarcely be a more fitting approach to the sacrament than this. It is a prayer in which we adjust ourselves to the presence of God and place our lives under his surveillance. As we do so we open our hearts to him and invoke the cleansing and renewing power of the Holy Spirit, so that our worship may be acceptable and may glorify the Lord.

The prayer falls into two sections. In the first part we frankly acknowledge that the God to whom we pray knows everything about us, and about every one of us, for he is the one to *whom all hearts be open, all desires known, and from whom no secrets are hid*. We cannot conceal anything from him, nor should we attempt to do so. Bishop Ken in his morning hymn urges us to remember this fact:

> Think how all-seeing God thy ways
> And all thy secret thoughts surveys.

Our hearts – that is, our inmost beings – are open to him. 'There is nothing in creation that can hide from him,' says the writer to the Hebrews; 'everything lies naked and exposed to the eyes of the One with whom we have to reckon' (4.13 NEB). We may deceive others, and we may even deceive ourselves, but we cannot deceive God; and it is with him that we have to reckon.

Again, to him 'all desires are known'. So Cranmer rendered the Latin *omnis voluntas loquitur*, which more literally means that to God 'every wish is eloquent'. It is a striking phrase. God is not only all-seeing but all-hearing, and each impulse of the will speaks to him. So, inevitably, from him 'no secrets are hid'.

Here then, in the first part of the collect, we are reminded of the divine omniscience, in order that (as Evan Daniel puts it) 'we may be led to see the futility of all our attempts to "dissemble and cloak" our sins and wickedness, and so be encouraged to make a complete confession, and obtain a complete absolution before communicating.'

The fact that we cannot hide anything from God, who sees all and knows all, may appear to be somewhat intimidating. But we may find a measure of comfort here as well. At least we haven't got to try to keep up appearances with God, as sometimes we have to with our friends and families. And again, there is no possibility of our being *mis*judged by him, as we may be by others. He knows us as we really are, and recognizes the good as well as the bad that is in us.

A familiar evening hymn speaks of God's 'kind but searching glance' which scans our lives; and it is well to remember, as Martin Parsons points out, that the searching glance is also kind. 'He sees the struggle in the heart, the desire for better things, the secret longing after holiness. We have nothing to fear if we are open with God.'[1]

We are being open with God as, in the second part of the collect, we go on to pray: *Cleanse the thoughts of our hearts by the inspiration of thy Holy Spirit*. Our hearts need his cleansing. Indeed, not merely our hearts as such, but the very *thoughts* of our hearts. What sort of thoughts do we harbour in our hearts? At times, almost certainly, proud thoughts, selfish thoughts, jealous thoughts. At other times maybe evil, hateful, impure thoughts. Well may we cry:

O God, make clean our hearts within us;
And take not thy Holy Spirit from us.

In the collect we pray for something better: not simply that God will not take his Holy Spirit from us, but that he will pour his Holy Spirit into us. This is the meaning of the original prayer. The Latin word is *infusionem*, which means inpouring. We are praying that the Spirit of purity and grace may cleanse our hearts and sanctify our lives, in order that, as the collect concludes, *we may perfectly love thee, and worthily magnify thy holy Name.*

To love God perfectly is to love him wholly, entirely. So this Collect for Purity has also been called the Collect for Singleness of heart (John W. Suter). The first and great commandment is that we should love God with all our heart and soul and mind and strength. The more fully we are able to obey it, the more 'worthily' (but not meritoriously, as the original prayer implied) shall we be able to 'magnify' the Lord – that is, to tell forth his greatness, as did Mary in her Magnificat (Luke 1.46 NEB).

On this high note the collect ends, and in this exalted spirit we enter upon our worship. Unworthy as we are in ourselves, we come to share in holy communion with the Lord and with his people, as those whose hearts and minds are hallowed by the Holy Spirit.

Note
[1] *The Holy Communion* (Hodder & Stoughton, 1961), p. 27.

The Prayer of Humble Access

We do not presume to come to this thy Table, O merciful Lord, trusting in our own righteousness, but in thy manifold and great mercies. We are not worthy so much as to gather up the crumbs under thy Table. But thou art the same Lord, whose property is always to have mercy: Grant us therefore, gracious Lord, so to eat the flesh of thy dear Son Jesus Christ, and to drink his blood, that our sinful bodies may be made clean by his body, and our souls washed through his most precious blood, and that we may evermore dwell in him, and he in us.

The title of this prayer comes from the Scottish Liturgy of 1637, where it is called 'Collect of Humble Access to the Holy Communion'. It first appeared in the Order of Holy Communion of 1548 and so came into the first English Prayer Book the following year. It was there placed after the Prayer of Consecration, immediately before the reception of the sacrament, and this would seem to be its most suitable position. The authorship of the prayer is obscure. Nothing definite can be said on the subject, but clearly the prayer was composed at the time of the Reformation.

Its purpose is to provide an answer to the question, In what spirit are we to approach the Lord's Table and partake of the sacrament? The answer is given first in negative terms. In fact there is a double negative: 'We do not presume . . .'; 'We are not worthy . . .'

We do not presume to come to the Lord's Table *trusting in our own righteousness*. That should be obvious enough, for the simple fact is, we have no righteousness of our own. To imagine that we have is sheer pride and presumption. The words of St Paul in Philippians 3.4–9 must have been in the author's mind at this point. Writing out of his past experience the apostle tells how, as a Jewish Pharisee, he had indeed trusted in his own righteousness, a righteousness achieved by his endeavours to keep the law; but how, as a Christian, he had abandoned all such efforts as worthless. He had only one desire now – to 'gain Christ, and be found in him, not having a righteousness of my own, based on law, but that which is through faith in Christ.'

We come to receive the Holy Communion with that same faith. Like the apostle, we do not trust in ourselves or what we have done. We cast ourselves upon the Lord's *manifold and great mercies*.

The second negative follows. *We are not worthy so much as to gather up the crumbs under thy Table*. The language here is borrowed from the story of Jesus and the Syrophoenician woman who had appealed to him for help (Mark 7.24–30). Jesus told her that it was not right to take the children's bread and cast it to the dogs. The 'children' were the Jews; the 'dogs' were the Gentiles. And the woman was a Gentile. But she splendidly rose to the challenge. 'Yes, Lord,' she replied, 'but even the dogs under the table eat the children's crumbs!'

Her faith was rewarded. The Lord gave her not the dog's crumbs but the children's bread. And he gives us the same, unworthy as we are. For now we are *all* the children of God through faith in Christ, whether Jew or Gentile, and we are dealing with *the same Lord, whose property* (i.e. essential character) *is always to have mercy*.

On this basis, recognizing our own unworthiness and the Lord's infinite mercy, we proceed to make our request: that we may *eat the flesh* and *drink the blood* of his *dear Son Jesus Christ*. The words have reference to our Lord's sacramental discourse in St John's Gospel: 'He who eats my flesh and drinks my blood has eternal life, and I will raise him up at the last day. For my flesh is food indeed, and my blood is drink indeed' (6.54, 55). We who in faith receive the bread and wine of the eucharist are partakers of the Lord's most blessed body and blood.

So far we are on safe scriptural ground. But what of the clauses in the prayer that follow, about *our sinful bodies* being *made clean by his body, and our souls washed through his most precious blood*? Here we must accept the fact that the prayer goes wrong. There is no biblical or theological warrant for drawing a distinction between the efficacy of the Lord's body and that of his blood, nor for associating his crucified body with the cleansing of our sinful bodies and his shed blood with the washing of our souls.

The Puritans at the Savoy Conference, 1661, rightly objected to this clause and proposed that it be altered to 'that our sinful souls and bodies may be cleansed through his precious body and blood.' This would have been more satisfactory; but unhappily the Bishops were not in a conciliatory mood and the proposal was not adopted in the 1662 Prayer Book. As it is, we have either to omit the words (as is done in the ASB) or accept their general intention, which is to make clear that the saving benefits of Christ's passion avail for our whole personality, body and soul alike.

There can be no dispute about the final words of the prayer: *that we may evermore dwell in him, and he in us*. Again the words of Jesus in John 6 are reflected: 'He who eats my flesh and drinks my blood abides in me and I in him' (v. 56). To meet with the risen Lord at his Table and feed upon him by faith with thanksgiving, is to enter into closer union with him and to know something more of his abiding presence in our lives.

Our Priestly Service

Prevent us, O Lord, in all our doings with thy most gracious favour, and further us with thy continual help; that in all our works, begun, continued, and ended in thee, we may glorify thy holy Name, and finally by thy mercy obtain everlasting life; through Jesus Christ our Lord.

Most Anglicans have probably heard this collect said dozens of times, for it is among the most familiar collects in the BCP. Yet it is safe to say that if we were to hear it a hundred times more it would never occur to us that it had anything particular to do with ordination and the priestly office.

Originally, however, the connection was a close one. The collect comes from the Gregorian Sacramentary, where it occurs as a prayer to be said on the Saturday before the Lent ordination and also at the end of the ordination service itself. This association was preserved in the Ordinal of the 1662 Prayer Book where the collect is found at the end of each of the three services. In the Sarum Missal it is the final prayer of the Mass, appointed to be said by the priest in private at the end of the service. This no doubt accounts for its place among the post-communion prayers in the BCP.

Clearly then the collect has connections with priesthood; but its use now is not restricted to the clergy. The whole Church is a 'royal priesthood' (1 Peter 2.9) and every Christian has a priestly ministry to fulfil as a member of the Body of Christ. So this is a prayer which we may all make our own in the service of God.

Prevent us, O Lord, in all our doings with thy most gracious favour. 'Prevent' is used in its older and original meaning of to precede or go before. The American Prayer Book substitutes 'Direct'; the ASB has 'Guide'. In this prayer we are asking the Lord to go ahead of us in all our endeavours, that we may follow where he leads. The initiative lies with him, not with us. The Israelites in their wilderness journey were guided on their way to the promised land by the pillar of cloud by day and the pillar of fire by night. Thus the Lord 'prevented' them in all their doings. We pray that he will do the same for us, and go before us with his 'most gracious favour': words which speak of his undeserved love and goodness to us his unworthy servants.

And further us with thy continual help. The original Latin of the prayer requests that God will 'follow us' with his help. This balances the previous petition. We ask not only that the Lord will lead us forward in his service and prepare the way for all that we have to do. We ask also that he will follow us with his aid and so enable us to accomplish what he wants done. The prayer is based on the conviction that God's callings are also his enablings.

Our purpose in making this request is expressed in the closing words of the collect: *that in all our works, begun, continued, and ended in thee, we may glorify thy holy Name* . . . How in fact do we begin, continue and end our works in God?

There is a prayer by Bishop George Hickes (1642–1715) which, slightly adapted, may suggest an answer, for it begins: 'Teach us, O gracious Lord, to begin our works with faith, to go on with obedience, and to finish them in love . . .' Faith is certainly the starting-point, as love is the crown, of all our efforts to serve God; and we continue in them by constant obedience to his word and will.

The ultimate goal is that we may glorify his holy name. We should have no other objective in view than that. In the works we do, we are not concerned to seek our own glory or to acquire merit. And therefore we are not, at this juncture, concerned that *finally* we may *obtain everlasting life*. I cannot but think that it is better for the last clause of the collect to be omitted. It introduces a foreign element into the prayer, that of self-interest. To serve God in the royal priesthood to which he has called us is the highest privilege that this life affords and brings its own reward. We ask nothing more for ourselves. Over all our service must be inscribed the words, *ad majorem Dei gloriam* – for the greater glory of God.

As a final point of interest it may be noted that this collect has much in common, both in language and contents, with the collect of the Seventeenth Sunday after Trinity in the BCP:

Lord, we pray thee that thy grace may always prevent and follow us, and make us continually to be given to all good works; through Jesus Christ our Lord.

The Advent Collect

Almighty God, give us grace that we may cast away the works of darkness, and put upon us the armour of light, now in the time of this mortal life, in which thy Son Jesus Christ came to visit us in great humility; that in the last day, when he shall come again in his glorious Majesty, to judge both the quick and the dead, we may rise to the life immortal; through him who liveth and reigneth with thee and the Holy Ghost, now and ever.

Advent marks the beginning of the Christian Year and is concerned with the coming of Christ to the world. The Advent collect accordingly takes up this theme. The rubric which follows it (added in 1662) directs that the collect 'is to be repeated with the other Collects in Advent, until Christmas Eve'.

The collect was composed for the 1549 Prayer Book and is generally assumed to have been written by Cranmer. Like all collects composed by the Reformers, it is strongly biblical in character. It is based on the latter part of the Epistle of the First Sunday in Advent, Romans 13.11–14.

The collect may be viewed as a study in contrasts. There are three of them, and the first is the contrast between darkness and light. *Almighty God, give us grace that we may cast away the works of darkness, and put upon us the armour of light.* The words are a direct quotation from the Epistle, in which St Paul is speaking of the Christian hope of salvation. 'Now is our salvation nearer than when we (first) believed,' he declares. 'The night is far spent, the day is at hand.' What then? The answer is: 'Let us therefore cast off the works of darkness, and let us put on the armour of light' (AV).

Here, as elsewhere, the apostle draws a distinction between the world's dark night and the glorious new day that has dawned for believers with the coming of Christ. Christians are children of light, children of the day (1 Thessalonians 5.5). They must therefore 'take no part in the barren deeds of darkness' but 'live like men who are at home in daylight' (Ephesians 5.8–10 NEB).

Here we are confronted with the moral demands of the gospel. We must 'cast away', like a polluted garment, the dark deeds of the old unregenerate life (things like drunkenness, debauchery, quarrelling, jealousy, mentioned in the Epistle). But having done that, we are not to leave matters there. A negative religion is of little value. We must also 'put on' something – 'the armour of light'. Not the robe of light, as we might have expected in view of the analogy, but the *armour*. There is a battle to be fought with the powers of darkness. We must be armed for war. But we cannot fight in our own strength, so the apostle's final exhortation is, 'Put ye on the Lord Jesus Christ', or as the NEB has it, 'Let Christ Jesus himself be the armour that you wear.'

The second contrast is between our mortal life and the life immortal. The Christian's struggle against the forces of evil is something that is going on now – *now in the time of this mortal life*. Our mortal life is the life we live in the present world and which is subject to death. We do not know how long it will last, but we do know that it will not last for ever; it is therefore right that we should reflect on that fact from time to time, so that we may use life to the full while it is ours.

The Bible attaches immense importance to the time of this mortal life, and teaches us to face it seriously and responsibly. For this life of ours, mortal though it be, is the only life we have in this world. We may employ it in the service of God and man, or squander it on the passing things of the world. To do the latter, Jesus warned us, is to lose our life – and it will be a total loss. Death when it comes will rob us of everything. But there is an alternative. We may deny self, take up our cross and follow Jesus; and then, *in the last day*, when this mortal existence is finished, we shall *rise to the life immortal*, the life which death cannot touch (see Mark 8.34–8).

The third contrast is between lowliness and majesty. When the Son of God entered this world and was born of the Virgin Mary, he *came to visit us in great humility*. The Incarnation was a supreme act of condescension. He who was rich, for our sakes became poor. The Lord of glory 'emptied himself' of the insignia of majesty (to use

Bishop Lightfoot's phrase) and was made in the likeness of men.

Now the contrast. When the Lord Jesus comes again, it will be *in his glorious majesty, to judge both the quick and the dead.* The same Christ who was born in poverty and obscurity at Bethlehem is coming in power and great glory at the consummation of human history. He is coming as King to establish his reign of righteousness and peace. But he is coming also as the Judge of mankind, both the living and the dead.

Judgement is one of the keynotes of Advent. This is what imparts to the season its solemn and penitential character. It calls us to examine ourselves – our conduct, our motives, our priorities, our ambitions – and so to prepare the way of the Lord in our own lives.

The Collect of the Nativity

Almighty God, who hast given us thy only-begotten Son to take our nature upon him, and as at this time to be born of a pure Virgin: Grant that we being regenerate, and made thy children by adoption and grace, may daily be renewed by thy Holy Spirit; through the same our Lord Jesus Christ, who liveth and reigneth with thee and the same Spirit, ever one God, world without end.

In the pre-Reformation Church provision was made for three celebrations of Holy Communion on Christmas Day, each with its own collect. The first of these was for the midnight mass on Christmas Eve, the collect (in the 1928 Prayer Book) beginning: 'God, who makest us glad with the yearly remembrance of the birth of thy only Son Jesus Christ'. The second celebration took place at daybreak and the collect was a prayer that 'the new light of the incarnate Word' might be enkindled in the hearts and shine forth in the lives of God's people.

The third collect, for the main celebration later in the morning, was basically the collect of the Nativity of our Lord as we have it in the BCP and in its revised form in the ASB. In the former it is prescribed for use both on Christmas Day itself and on the following Sunday. Cranmer considerably revised and amplified the original Latin version and gave it a more biblical character. It is clearly based on the Epistle appointed for the Sunday after Christmas, Galatians 4.1–7, the latter part of which reads:

> When the time had fully come, God sent forth his Son, born of a woman, born under the law, to redeem those who were under the law, so that we might receive adoption as sons. And because you are sons, God has sent the Spirit of his Son into our hearts, crying, 'Abba! Father!'

There are a number of ideas in the collect. The primary and dominant theme, rightly enough, is that of the Incarnation, not simply the historical fact of the Nativity. Something astonishing happened at the first Christmas. God gave his *only-begotten Son to take our nature upon him, and to be born of a pure Virgin*. In the words of the Epistle: 'When the time had fully come, God sent forth his Son, born of a woman'.

This was God's decisive hour, the supreme moment of human history. He who was born in the stable at Bethlehem was the eternal and pre-existent Son of God who, as such, already possessed the divine nature. Now, as the collect affirms, he took upon him our human nature by being born of a human mother. In doing so he assumed all that was essential to our humanity. As Bishop Masterman remarks, 'He did not assume a sinful nature, for sin is no part of a true human nature. Jesus Christ was not a man who became Divine, but the Divine become man. The Incarnation was not first the ennobling of man, but the condescension of God.'

This is the ultimate truth we celebrate at Christmas, the truth of God incarnate. 'The Word became flesh.' Into that deep mystery the human mind cannot fully penetrate; but where reason fails, faith accepts and love adores.

The next theme in the collect is that of regeneration, or new birth. A parallel is drawn between the historical birth of Jesus and our spiritual rebirth by water and the Spirit. The collect speaks of our *being regenerate, and made thy* (God's) *children by adoption and grace*. Corresponding to this is the statement in the Epistle that God's purpose in sending his Son was to redeem us so 'that we might receive adoption as sons'. Our Lord's birth into the human family makes possible our new birth into the heavenly family. He was

Born to raise the sons of earth,
Born to give them second birth.

It is important to grasp that as Christians we are 'regenerate and made God's children' not by any effort or virtue of our own, but entirely by God's grace. He has 'adopted' us as his own out of his boundless, unmerited love in Jesus Christ (John 1.12, 13). Baptism is the sacramental expression and seal of our regeneration and confers upon us the status of the children of God. But in actual experience the new birth is not simply a change of status. It is a change of heart, a new life; for the Son of God took our nature upon him so that we might become partakers of his divine nature.

That brings us to the third keyword of the collect, which is sanctification. At this point it relates to our everyday life. Our prayer is that, as children of God, we *may daily be renewed by thy Holy Spirit*. The Epistle states: 'Because you are sons, God has sent the Spirit of his Son into our hearts, crying, "Abba! Father!"'

The prayer is not that we may *receive* the Spirit. That has already happened in the new birth. It is a prayer that we may be *renewed* by the Spirit from day to day: renewed in love for God and one another, renewed in faith and hope, renewed in power for the service of Christ's kingdom. This is a continuous and ongoing process, the work of God's Holy Spirit. And this is true sanctification.

The collect has a strong theological content and character. But its aim is practical: the spiritual renewal of the Church and all its members, ourselves included. And it ends on a note of glory in the ascription. The same Lord Jesus who was born in a stable and laid in a manger, now lives and reigns in heaven, in the unity of the Father and the Holy Spirit, *ever one God, world without end*. So, as it has been said, from the manger of Bethlehem we look up to the throne of God.

The Lenten Collect

Almighty and everlasting God, who hatest nothing that thou hast made, and dost forgive the sins of all them that are penitent: Create and make in us new and contrite hearts, that we worthily lamenting our sins, and acknowledging our wretchedness, may obtain of thee, the God of all mercy, perfect remission and forgiveness; through Jesus Christ our Lord.

The Collect of Ash Wednesday is directed in the BCP to be read every day in Lent. This imparts to it a seasonal character. Its two dominant themes are the distinctive notes of Lent, namely penitence and forgiveness: penitence on our part, and forgiveness on God's.

The collect was composed for the 1549 Prayer Book. It was not an entirely new prayer, for the opening invocation is very similar to that of the ancient Latin collect which it replaced. But the latter part of the prayer is quite different from the old, which asked that God's faithful people might 'enter upon this solemn fast with becoming piety, and go through it with unmolested devotion.' Contrast that, says Dyson Hague, with the present collect, 'with its searching spirituality and its exquisite tenderness of evangelical tone.'

The invocation is based on words from the Wisdom of Solomon in the Apocrypha: 'Thou hast mercy on all men . . . and thou overlookest the sins of men to the end they may repent. For thou lovest all things that are, and abhorrest none of the things which thou didst make' (11.23–4).

Some may think, as I do, that it would have been preferable for the collect to begin on a positive rather than a negative note and to incorporate the words about God 'loving all things' rather than 'hating nothing' he has made. The collect might then begin:

'Almighty and everlasting God, who lovest everything that thou hast made, and dost forgive the sins . . .'

The biblical doctrine of the forgiveness of sins is rooted in the love of God, the love which found visible expression in the Cross. 'God has shown how much he loves us: it was while we were still sinners that Christ died for us' (Romans 5.8 GNB). God never ceases to love the sinner while hating his sin; and that means that we too must hate sin and be truly *penitent* if we are to receive his forgiveness.

What is repentance? It is said that Frederick Temple, when Bishop of London, once asked that question of a class of children he was examining in the catechism. A child answered, 'A heart broken because of sin.' 'No!' replied the bishop in his abrupt manner, 'it is a heart broken away from sin.'

Penitence means more than being sorry for sin. It is not just an emotional experience. It means to renounce and forsake sin, to have done with it. So in the end it is a matter of amendment. And that is not easy. It is not something we can achieve by our own efforts. The petition that follows in the collect makes that clear.

Create and make in us new and contrite hearts. God alone can do that; he is the Creator. The language is taken from David's penitential prayer in Psalm 51: 'Create in me a clean heart, O God, and renew a right spirit within me.' And again: 'A broken and a contrite heart, O God, thou wilt not despise' (vv.10, 17 AV).

The emphasis in the collect is on the word contrite. The new heart for which we pray is a heart that is truly penitent, the heart that is ours when we are *worthily lamenting our sins, and acknowledging our wretchedness*.

'We lament our sins *worthily*,' comments Leo Stephens-Hodge, 'when we forsake them for what they are in themselves, an affront against God's holiness and love, and not merely for the trouble they may give us afterwards. *Wretchedness* means the unhappiness which is the result of sin.'

When our penitence is thus genuine we may confidently expect our prayer to be answered, and to obtain of God, *the God of all mercy, perfect remission and forgiveness*. The last two words are not entirely synonymous. They each take a different view of sin. As a debt, sin needs to be *remitted*; as an offence, it needs to be *forgiven*. In his matchless grace God freely remits the vast debt we owe and could never pay (Matthew 18.23–35), and in the same way he fully forgives all our offences, for Christ's sake (Ephesians 4.32).

This collect, it will be recognized, is deeply introspective, and introspection has its perils. It is not a good or healthy thing to keep on searching our hearts and dwelling on our shortcomings. But there are times when we should do this, and Lent is one of those times. It calls us to engage in some spiritual stocktaking, to see ourselves as we really are, and to take sin seriously.

Some words of Francis Wheeler in his Ash Wednesday reflection are worth pondering in this connection. 'So long as sin remains undisturbed, external self-denial is more or less futile. Mind and desire must first be turned away from this thing God hates: only then do we begin to enter on the way of penitence, and only true penitence can obtain the divine forgiveness for which we so often pray during Lent.'[1]

Note

[1] *Prayer Book Meditations* (Mowbray 1961), p. 30.

The Easter Collect

Almighty God, who through thine only-begotten Son Jesus Christ hast overcome death, and opened unto us the gate of everlasting life: We humbly beseech thee, that as by thy special grace preventing us thou dost put into our minds good desires, so by thy continual help we may bring the same to good effect; through Jesus Christ our Lord, who liveth and reigneth with thee and the Holy Ghost, ever one God, world without end.

In the form in which it appears in the BCP, the Easter collect cannot be regarded as wholly satisfactory. The opening invocation is splendid; the prayer which follows is disappointing, since it makes no specific reference to the Lord's resurrection or its significance for our lives. There is much to be said for the additional Easter collect provided in the 1928 Prayer Book. Taken from the Gregorian Sacramentary, it was appointed in the first English Prayer Book (1549) for use on Easter Day 'in the mornyng, afore Mattyns'. It was printed thus:

> O God, who for our redempcion dyddest geue thyne only begotten sonne to the death of the Crosse: and by his glorious resurrection haste delyuered us from the power of our enemye: Graunte us so to dye daylye from synne, that we may euermore lyue with hym in the ioy of hys resurreccion; through the same Christe our Lorde.

The difficulty with our Easter collect is that it is really a mixture of two ancient collects. The first, in the Sacramentary of Gelasius, began with the same invocation as ours, but continued: 'Grant, we beseech thee, that we who celebrate the festival of the Lord's resurrection may, through the renewal of thy Spirit, rise from the death of the soul.' This makes a quite suitable prayer. However, in the slightly later Gregorian Sacramentary the petition was altered to the form in which we now have it. The alteration, with its reference to God's 'special grace preventing us', was made to counteract the Pelagian heresy, which taught that man is capable of pleasing God by his own unaided efforts, apart from divine grace. We may agree that sound doctrine is important; but we may also question whether Easter Day is the occasion to embark upon a heresy hunt. The original version of the collect is to be preferred.

In the ASB the first collect of Easter Day is an attempt to provide a modern prayer more worthy of the Queen of Festivals. The second is simply the Prayer Book collect recast in modern form. An alternative version might be one which embodies in the petition the opening words of the Epistle (Colossians 3.1–7), thus: 'Grant that we, being risen with him, may seek the things that are above, where he lives and reigns with you and the Holy Spirit, one God, now and for ever.'

As for the collect in its Prayer Book form, we may note three things. First, as the splendid invocation triumphantly affirms, God has *overcome death* through the resurrection of his Son *and opened unto us the gate of everlasting life*. The Easter Even collect speaks of the gate of *death*; but for us who believe in Jesus Christ the gate of death is the gate of life through which we pass to our joyful resurrection. Death is not the end of life. It is the beginning of Life – the life which has no end. Such is our Easter faith.

Jesus lives! henceforth is death
But the gate of life immortal.

Secondly, we note what we are asking God to do for us when we pray that by his *special grace preventing us* he will *put into our minds good desires*. This is what theologians call God's 'prevenient grace', the grace which goes before us and inclines our hearts to seek what is good. In the words of Bishop Masterman: 'Quite simply expressed, prevenient grace means that we need God before we are conscious of our need, and that God helps us before we learn to recognize his help.'

In the third place, the collect reminds us that just as God kindles 'good desires' within our hearts, so by his *continual help* he enables us to bring them to *good effect*. At this point an attempt may be made to link the words of the collect to the message of Easter.

What are we to understand by 'good effect'? Surely the phrase indicates among other things that as believers in the resurrection of Jesus we should be effective Christians. Certainly the resurrection faith is an effective faith. It is as relevant for life as it is for death, for this present world as for the world to come. The apostle Paul asserts that the vast resources of divine power which raised Christ from the dead are open to us who trust in him (Ephesians 1.18, 19). Thus it is that the God of all grace works in us, 'inspiring both the will and the deed, for his own chosen purpose' (Philippians 2.13 NEB).

The Whitsun Collect

God, who as at this time didst teach the hearts of thy faithful people, by the sending to them the light of thy Holy Spirit: Grant us by the same Spirit to have a right judgement in all things, and evermore to rejoice in his holy comfort; through the merits of Christ Jesus our Saviour, who liveth and reigneth with thee, in the unity of the same Spirit, one God, world without end.

The collect appointed for Whitsunday, or the feast of Pentecost, concentrates almost exclusively on one aspect of the Holy Spirit's operations, namely his teaching office. Many other aspects of his work are stressed in the New Testament, but his ministry as the teacher of the faithful finds particular expression in the words of Jesus in the Gospel of the day (John 14.15–31). Thus: 'I will pray the Father, and he shall give you another Counsellor, to be with you for ever, even the Spirit of truth' (v. 16). And again: 'The Counsellor, the Holy Spirit, whom the Father will send in my name, he will teach you all things, and bring to your remembrance all that I have said to you' (v. 26). Our Lord's later teaching in the same discourse amplifies this (ch. 16.13–15).

The collect, which comes from the Gregorian Sacramentary, is unusual in beginning with the single word *God*, without further definition – a usage found nowhere else in the Prayer Book. The opening words look back to what happened on the day of Pentecost and its significance for the Church. God taught his *faithful people by the sending to them the light of (his) Holy Spirit*.

Light, in the Bible, is the symbol of truth and knowledge, just as darkness represents error and ignorance. So the Holy Spirit, as the Spirit of truth, is the Illuminator of the Church. He teaches the hearts of the faithful. The word hearts is used in the collect not in contrast to the intellect (for the Spirit illuminates both faculties) but rather to indicate the inwardness of his operations. 'I will put my law within them, and I will write it upon their hearts' is the promise of the new covenant (Jeremiah 31.33). The Holy Spirit is the true Inner Light on which the Society of Friends places such emphasis. Hence our prayer to the Paraclete must constantly be:

> O thou blessèd Light divine,
> Shine within these hearts of thine,
> And our inmost being fill.

In keeping with this, two petitions follow in relation to the Holy Spirit. The first is: *Grant us by the same Spirit to have a right judgement in all things*. The words 'in all things' were added to the collect by the Reformers 'to bring out more clearly the completeness of our dependence on the teaching of the Holy Spirit' (J. H. B. Masterman). In asking that the Holy Spirit may give us 'a right judgement' we are seeking something more than sanctified common sense. True spiritual discernment is what is meant. And such discernment is what we need if we are to gain a clear understanding of the truth, to make wise decisions in the crises of our lives, and to perceive in every situation what is the good and acceptable and perfect will of God. Our prayer to him will be: 'Teach me to do thy will, for thou art my God! Let thy good Spirit lead me on a level path!' (Psalm 143.10).

The second petition relating to the Holy Spirit is that we may *evermore rejoice in his holy comfort*. There are two ways of understanding the word comfort. We now think of it in its modern sense of consolation; but its old and original meaning was that of fortification, for it has its root in the Latin *fortis*, meaning courageous, brave, strong.

The Holy Spirit is both Comforter and Fortifier or Helper, as Bishop Michael Ramsey points out in his book *Holy Spirit*.[1] He consoles God's people by making the presence of Christ real to them, so that they are not left desolate or orphans (John 14.18). He fortifies them by strengthening them with might in their inner being (Ephesians 3.16) and empowering them for witness in the world (Acts 1.8). In both senses we may rejoice in the Spirit's holy comfort.

The collects of the three major festivals of Christmas, Easter and

Pentecost all end with a Trinitarian doxology. Hence the conclusion to the present collect: *through the merits of Christ Jesus our Saviour, who liveth and reigneth with thee, in the unity of the same Spirit, one God, world without end*. This form of ending is distinctive and is not found elsewhere in the BCP. In concluding the Whitsun collect it provides a fitting prelude to Trinity Sunday.

Note

[1]Michael Ramsey, *Holy Spirit* (SPCK, 1977), pp. 103–7.

The Collect of All Saints' Day

O Almighty God, who hast knit together thine elect in one communion and fellowship, in the mystical body of thy Son Christ our Lord: Grant us grace so to follow thy blessed Saints in all virtuous and godly living, that we may come to those unspeakable joys, which thou hast prepared for them that unfeignedly love thee; through Jesus Christ our Lord.

Saints' days are not as widely observed by church people now as they used to be. Whatever may be the reason for that, there are happily certain exceptions, and All Saints' Day is one of them. This great Christian festival, dating back to the fourth century, still has a popular appeal, and in the minds of many its appeal is enhanced by the splendid collect which crystallizes its meaning and message.

The collect was written by Cranmer for the 1549 Prayer Book. The old Sarum collect which it replaced was concerned with the veneration of all the saints and the multiplicity of their intercessions for the Church on earth. For obvious reasons this did not commend itself to the Reformers, and a collect of a more biblical character was called for.

The collect falls into two parts. The first is a thankful commemoration of the communion of saints; the second a prayer that we may be given grace to tread in their steps and partake at last of their joy.

We ought to be clear at the outset what we mean by the communion of saints. It may help if we remember that in the Apostles' Creed the phrase is used in immediate association with the holy Catholic Church. It emphasizes one particular aspect of the Church: the fellowship which unites all who are *knit together* in Christ and who form his *mystical body*, that is, his spiritual body (see Ephesians 4.16). They are designated in the collect as God's *elect*, which like the term *saints* itself is simply a name given in the New Testament to all Christians without distinction. In other words, the 'elect' and the 'saints' are synonymous with the Church.

The fellowship or communion (*koinonia*) which Christians enjoy one with another has two notable features. For one thing, it recognizes no differences of race, colour, class or sex. In Christ all are equal and all are one (Galatians 3.28). The other thing is that, being 'in Christ', the fellowship is independent of time and space, and not even death itself can break it.

> One family we dwell in him,
> One Church, above, beneath,
> Though now divided by the stream,
> The narrow stream of death.

There is deep comfort in the thought of the communion of saints as we remember the departed. Since we are in fellowship with Christ, we are in fellowship with them also.

The second part of the prayer links up directly with the saintly company and looks to the eternal future. *Grant us grace so to follow thy blessed Saints in all virtuous and godly living, that we may come to those unspeakable joys, which thou hast prepared for them that unfeignedly love thee.*

Note the word *grace*. The collect is not teaching a doctrine of salvation by works, as though by our 'virtuous and godly living' we may merit a place in heaven. The blessed saints themselves whom we seek to follow contradict any such idea. All that they were, and all that they achieved, was by the grace of God. We ask the same grace for ourselves. Just as we are saved by grace, and serve and please God by grace, so by his grace we shall come at last to the unspeakable joys of heaven.

God is preparing those joys 'for them that unfeignedly love him'. To love God unfeignedly is to love him sincerely, genuinely, without pretence. This is what St Paul had in mind when he saluted 'all them that love our Lord Jesus Christ in sincerity' (Ephesians 6.24 AV) – that is, as the Greek indicates, with a love that is incorruptible.

The unutterable joys of heaven are not reserved for an exclusive few whose love for God was perfect. They are for all whose love is real, and who can say from the heart like Simon Peter, 'Lord, you know everything; you know that I love you' (John 21.17).

Heaven, it has been said, is a prepared place for a prepared people. As God is preparing the place for us, so may he prepare us for the place. The communion of saints is wonderful. The company of the saints will be more wonderful still.

The Prayer for Unity

O God, the Father of our Lord Jesus Christ, our only Saviour, the Prince of Peace: Give us grace seriously to lay to heart the great dangers we are in by our unhappy divisions. Take away all hatred and prejudice, and whatsoever else may hinder us from godly union and concord: that, as there is but one Body, and one Spirit, and one hope of our calling, one Lord, one faith, one baptism, one God and Father of us all; so we may henceforth be all of one heart, and of one soul, united in one holy bond of truth and peace, of faith and charity, and may with one mind and one mouth glorify thee; through Jesus Christ our Lord.

Forms of prayer to be used on the anniversary of the accession of the reigning sovereign have been in use in this country since 1576. From time to time they have undergone a fair amount of revision, especially in the earlier period. The existing orders of service will be found at the end of the BCP, before the Articles.

The services are now little used, and probably most church people are not even aware of their existence. But among them there is one liturgical gem, the Prayer for Unity, which was added to the services in 1715, at the accession of the House of Hanover. Its authorship is unknown.

The prayer falls into three parts. In the opening section attention is drawn to the need for unity and the urgent importance of achieving it. We frankly acknowledge *our unhappy divisions*, and such indeed they are. Yet merely to call them 'unhappy' is a vast understatement. They are tragic and shameful. They dishonour the name of Christ, *our only Saviour, the Prince of Peace*, whom we all profess to serve; they tarnish the image of the Church in the eyes of the world; and they give the lie to the gospel of reconciliation which we preach – preach, but apparently do not practise.

These things ought not so to be, and surely we cannot be content that they should continue. Hence the force of the prayer we offer: *Give us grace seriously to lay to heart the great dangers we are in* as a result of our divisions. The trouble is that we do not seriously lay to heart the scandal of a divided Christendom and the stupidity of our rival denominations. We have become so accustomed to the situation that we are inclined to accept it. We need to cast away our complacency and to show a far greater concern.

What is the cause of our divisions? The next section of the prayer points to the answer: *Take away all hatred and prejudice, and whatsoever else may hinder us from godly union and concord.* There can be no place or excuse for hatred between Christians of different persuasions. Yet we cannot deny that such hatred has existed in the past and still does exist to some extent; and it usually springs from prejudice: from small-mindedness and a one-sided view of the truth.

There is room for diversity within the Church. We cannot all agree with one another on every point of doctrine and practice. But however much we disagree, we must rid ourselves of bitterness and bigotry, of intolerance and uncharitableness, of an exclusive, sectarian spirit. These are the things that hinder us from godly union and concord. John Wesley, in his notable *Letter to a Roman Catholic* (1749), declared:

> If we cannot as yet *think* alike in all things, at least we may *love* alike. Herein we cannot possibly do amiss. For of one point none can doubt a moment: God is love, and he that dwelleth in love, dwelleth in God, and God in him.

In the last and longest part of the prayer we are reminded that the unity for which we pray is in accordance with the apostolic teaching: 'There is one body and one Spirit, just as you were called to the one hope that belongs to your call, one Lord, one faith, one baptism, one God and Father of us all' (Ephesians 4.4–6).

This sevenfold unity is something 'given', something that already exists, as the prayer recognizes in repeating the words. The *one Body* is the Body of Christ, the Church in its entirety. The *one Spirit* is the Holy Spirit who indwells the body and makes it a living organism. The *one hope* is the hope of glory, the eternal hope of all

God's people. The *one Lord* is the Lord Jesus, the central fact of this unity and also the secret of it. The *one faith* represents our response to the one Lord, and the *one baptism* is the visible seal, the sign that God has accepted us as his own. And this God is the *one God and Father of us all*, that is, of all of us Christians, whatever label we bear.

It is against this background that we pray that *we may henceforth be all of one heart, and of one soul, united in one holy bond of truth and peace, of faith and charity*. To be of one heart and soul is to be spiritually united; and the bond that unites us is not simply that of peace and charity but of truth and faith. This is significant. Unity between Christians and churches lies solely within the truth of the gospel and can be enjoyed only by the sharing of a common faith. It cannot be achieved in any other way.

Our final petition is this, that we *may with one mind and one mouth glorify thee*. The glory of God is the ultimate goal of our quest for unity. It should also be our all-compelling motive. The prayer echoes St Paul's words: 'God grant you to be likeminded one toward another according to Christ Jesus, that you may with one mind and one mouth glorify the God and Father of our Lord Jesus Christ' (Romans 15.5, 6).

The General Thanksgiving

Almighty God, Father of all mercies, we thine unworthy servants do give thee most humble and hearty thanks for all thy goodness and loving-kindness to us, and to all men. We bless thee for our creation, preservation, and all the blessings of this life; but above all for thine inestimable love in the redemption of the world by our Lord Jesus Christ, for the means of grace, and for the hope of glory. And we beseech thee, give us that due sense of all thy mercies, that our hearts may be unfeignedly thankful, and that we shew forth thy praise, not only with our lips, but in our lives; by giving up ourselves to thy service, and by walking before thee in holiness and righteousness all our days; through Jesus Christ our Lord, to whom with thee and the Holy Ghost be all honour and glory, world without end.

It is noteworthy that the General Thanksgiving in the BCP has passed into the ASB almost unchanged, apart from the alteration of the personal pronouns to their modern form. This is testimony to the timeless character of the prayer. It is as suitable for the twentieth century as it was for the seventeenth when it was composed for the 1662 Prayer Book. Its author was Dr Edward Reynolds, who was Bishop of Norwich 1661–76.

It is a remarkable piece of writing. On the one hand it is short enough to be easily memorized and simple enough to be readily understood. On the other hand it is sufficiently comprehensive to fulfil all the requirements of an act of thanksgiving suitable for use on almost any occasion. It is always an impressive experience to hear the familiar words recited by a company of church people who are able to join spontaneously in the prayer when called upon to do so.

It falls naturally into three sections, which in turn answer the basic questions which arise in connection with thanksgiving. Why should we give thanks? For what should we give thanks? How should we give thanks?

As regards the first question, the reason why we give thanks is made immediately clear in the opening words: *Almighty God, Father of all mercies*. That God is Almighty we accept as a matter of course. But that is not all. The marvellous thing is that the Almighty Creator is also the all-merciful Father. He is the Father of all mercies, and our thanksgiving springs from the recognition of that fact.

Next, as the recipients of his mercy, we confess ourselves to be his *unworthy servants*. We are not worthy to be called his servants, let alone to be called his sons. But the Lord deals with his servants not according to their merits but according to his mercy. Hence the thanks we offer him are both *humble and hearty*: humble because of our unworthiness, hearty because of our indebtedness. Who can estimate what we owe to God for *all* his *goodness and loving-kindness*, not only *to us* but *to all men*? Those last three words are significant. Our thanksgiving should not be narrow or self-centred. Just as we must pray for the things that others need, so we ought to give thanks for the blessings which others have received.

The second question is, For what should we give thanks? The answer is in the central part of the prayer, which provides a sort of agenda for thanksgiving. It spells out in general terms what the Father of all mercies in his goodness and loving-kindness has done for his children.

It begins on the material or human level. *We bless thee for our creation*. It is he that made us, and we are his (Psalm 100.3). The life we possess is his gift. Every breath we draw we owe to him. 'In him we live and move and have our being' (Acts 17.28). Furthermore, he has made us in his own image, and he has made us for himself, so that we are not simply physical beings, with bodies that are fearfully and wonderfully made, and rational beings with astonishing powers of intellect, but above all spiritual beings with the capacity to know and love and serve our Creator.

We also bless God for our *preservation*. He not only bestows on us the gift of life. He sustains the life that he has given. Some of us have been preserved through many years to a good old age. We have been preserved amid many dangers, known and unknown, including in all probability times of war. We have been preserved in our travels by land and sea and air. We have been preserved in days of illness, perhaps critical illness, when life itself hung in the balance. We would do well to reflect on these things when we bless God for our preservation.

And then we thank him for *all the blessings of this life*. Here is something else to think about. We are sometimes told to count our blessings, but in fact it is an impossible task. It is like trying to count the stars. No computer could ever enumerate all the blessings that this life affords us.

The greatest of those blessings are not the things that the world regards as of the highest worth – things such as money, possessions, pleasure, success, fame. If we get our priorities right we shall begin rather with matters like health, our physical and mental faculties, with the joys of home and family life, with the gifts of love and friendship, with the wonder of the world of nature and the beauty of earth and sea and sky. And what of the great enrichment we gain through music, art, and literature, through games and hobbies and recreation – yes, and through work?

Even so, the blessings of this life are not the greatest of God's gifts. There is something more, and something higher. *Above all*, says the prayer; and at this point we are lifted from the material to the spiritual level. Above all we bless God for his *inestimable love in the redemption of the world by our Lord Jesus Christ, for the means of grace, and for the hope of glory*. This, as it has been rightly said, is the focal point of the General Thanksgiving. Three keywords of our Christian religion – redemption, grace, and hope – are brought to our notice, related respectively to the past, the present, and the future.

First and foremost we bless God for his inestimable love, love so vast as to be beyond all human measurement. But what cannot be estimated has been demonstrated, and demonstrated in the most clear and decisive manner in the saving work of the Cross. This is what is meant by the redemption of the world. Our Lord Jesus Christ, by his perfect sacrifice and triumphant resurrection, has vanquished the power of death and freed us from the slavery of sin. It is an accomplished fact. It is God's doing, not ours. As William Temple wrote, 'All is of God; the only thing of my own which I can contribute to my own redemption is the sin from which I need to be redeemed.'

From the past we move into the present as we give thanks to God for the means of grace. It is by his grace that our Christian life is sustained from day to day. And grace is God in his graciousness imparting his love and power to us. The means or channels through which he does this are many, but it is always the same gracious God who is at work in us by his Spirit. The sacraments and the scriptures, worship and prayer, sermons and retreats, the fellowship of the Church in all its varied aspects – these are all means of grace by which we grow into spiritual maturity as members of the Body of Christ.

And as to the future – the hope of glory! It's all this and heaven too! Whatever we experience of God's grace in this life is as nothing compared with the glory that awaits us hereafter. 'Now we see as in a mirror dimly,' says St Paul, 'but then face to face' (1 Corinthians 13.12). Face to face with God! It is a staggering thought. 'His servants shall worship him,' wrote St John as he caught a glimpse of the City of God; but not only shall they worship him: 'they shall see his face' (Revelation 22.3, 4). The hope of glory is nothing less than the beatific vision.

In the light of all this, *how* are we to give thanks? The final part of the prayer supplies the answer. And the answer will be determined in the first instance by our having a *due sense of all (God's) mercies*: a deep and genuine appreciation of what in his goodness he has done for us. To that end we pray *that our hearts may be unfeignedly thankful, and that we may shew forth (God's) praise, not only with our lips, but in our lives*.

In those words, three agencies of thanksgiving are mentioned. (Incidentally, you will observe that the General Thanksgiving is fond of threes.) First there is the *heart*, for that is where true gratitude begins. It must be experienced inside of us before it can be expressed on the outside.

Secondly, we shew forth God's praise with our *lips*. True, not only with our lips but certainly with our lips as well. If our hearts are thankful, let us tell the Lord so – and tell others too. If he has given us voices to sing his praise, let us not keep silent.

Thirdly, we must praise him in our *lives*, and this is how: *by giving up ourselves to (his) service, and by walking before (him) in holiness and righteousness all our days*. Our praise is visible as well as vocal. It is seen as well as heard; and it is seen in dedicated service and holy living, in what we are and in what we do.

The Scottish churchman and poet, Horatius Bonar (1808–89), summed up the closing lines of this great prayer of thanksgiving in his fine hymn, 'Fill thou my life, O Lord my God, In every part with praise':

> Not for the lip of praise alone,
> Nor e'en the praising heart,
> I ask, but for a life made up
> Of praise in every part.
>
> Praise in the common things of life,
> Its goings out and in,
> Praise in each duty and each deed,
> However small and mean.

As Bishop J. Taylor Smith used to say, thanksgiving is good, but thanksliving is better.

The Benediction

The peace of God, which passeth all understanding, keep your hearts and minds in the knowledge and love of God, and of his Son Jesus Christ our Lord: and the blessing of God Almighty, the Father, the Son, and the Holy Ghost, be amongst you and remain with you always.

The sacramental hour is over – 'the hour of banquet and of song', as Horatius Bonar puts it in his communion hymn. We have accepted the Lord's invitation and obeyed his command. We have received the bread and wine and have fed by faith on the Body and Blood of Christ. We have enjoyed fellowship (*koinonia*) with him and with his people. Now we await the word of dismissal.

It comes in the familiar and much loved benediction, which sends us out into the world with the assurance that God's own peace and heavenly blessing go with us, and will abide with us always.

We may compare this Christian benediction with the Aaronic blessing in Numbers 6.24–6:

> The Lord bless you and keep you:
> The Lord make his face to shine upon you,
> and be gracious to you:
> The Lord lift up his countenance upon you,
> and give you peace.

The Jewish blessing ends with peace. The Christian blessing begins with it: *The peace of God, which passeth all understanding, keep your hearts and minds in the knowledge and love of God, and of his Son Jesus Christ our Lord*. The words are based on what St Paul wrote to the Philippian Christians after urging them to be anxious about nothing and prayerful about everything. 'And the peace of God, which passes all understanding, will keep your hearts and minds in Christ Jesus' (Philippians 4.7).

There are many things in life which we cannot understand but which we can nevertheless experience. The peace of God is one of these – the very peace which he himself possesses as the God of peace. And since it is *God's* peace, it transcends our finite understanding.

The apostle says that this peace will *keep* our hearts and minds in Christ. The verb has a military ring about it. It means to guard, to act as sentinel. In employing the word in that sense the benediction invokes God's peace to garrison our inner being, so that no foe may gain admission, either to distort our knowledge of God or diminish our love for him.

To know God is to love him. It is impossible to love him without knowing him. The better we know him the more we shall love him. Perhaps there is a connection between our knowledge and love of God on the one hand, and our hearts and minds on the other, as Evan Daniel suggests. 'As the mind is the seat of knowledge, so the heart is the seat of love.'

And the blessing of God Almighty, the Father, the Son, and the Holy Ghost, be amongst you and remain with you always. Little comment is called for here. We note that the blessing is invoked upon us as the worshipping congregation: it is essentially corporate in character. But it is not only to be among us while we thus meet together: it is to remain with us always. Above all, it is the blessing of the Almighty God, the holy and glorious Trinity: the Father, the Son, and the Holy Spirit.

If we inquire further into what such a benediction means, we may find an answer in Prayer Book words which are equally familiar, a prayer we often repeat together at the end of divine service:

> The grace of our Lord Jesus Christ, and the love of God, and the fellowship of the Holy Ghost, be with us all evermore.

The words come directly from the Scriptures, being the final verse of the second epistle to the Corinthians (13.14). It is the only Trinitarian form of blessing in the New Testament. Note what it says.

The blessing of God the Father is that of divine *love*: love for the lost, the lowest, and the least.

The blessing of God the Son is that of saving *grace*: the grace of forgiveness, freedom, peace, eternal life.

The blessing of God the Holy Spirit is that of creative *fellowship*: the fellowship of the Church in which all are equal and all are one in Christ.

The order of the clauses in the 'Grace' is not the traditional theological order. It is the order of Christian experience. Dr Donald Coggan admirably explains this when he writes:

> Times without number in the story of men's search for reality, beginning with the historic fact of Jesus Christ, the 'grace' of his Person and work, men have been led on to dare to believe in the love of God and in that fellowship of the Holy Spirit which finds its chief expression in the Church of God. God moves men, and brings them to himself, in an infinite number of ways. There is no set order or stereotyped pattern. But very often it proves to be the case that Christ's grace is the doorway, the entrance-gate, to a man's realization of God's love and the Spirit's fellowship.[1]

Note

[1] *The Prayers of the New Testament* (Hodder & Stoughton, 1967), p. 117.

Three

THE PATTERN PRAYER

Introducing the Lord's Prayer

Without question the best known words in the whole Bible are the Lord's Prayer as recorded in Matthew 6.9–13. Literally millions of people throughout the world can repeat the words in their mother tongue, churchgoers and non-churchgoers alike. Those who know no other verses of Scripture know these. Those who say no other prayer say this one. The prayer has a timeless and universal appeal. It is adapted to people of all races, all classes, all ages. It is the prayer Jesus himself gave us. That is why we call it the Lord's Prayer and that is why it possesses a unique value.

In this introductory chapter I invite you to look first at the setting of the prayer in St Matthew's Gospel. It is part of the Sermon on the Mount and comes from a section in which Jesus is dealing with the three religious duties of almsgiving, prayer and fasting (6.1–18). He begins by laying down a basic principle:

> 'Beware of practising your piety before men in order to be seen by them; for then you will have no reward from your Father who is in heaven.'

In applying this principle to the subject of prayer he gives his disciples a twofold warning. The first is this:

> 'When you pray, you must not be like the hypocrites; for they love to stand and pray in the synagogues and at the street corners, that they may be seen by men. Truly, I say to you, they have their reward' (v. 5).

By the hypocrites Jesus evidently meant the Pharisees, who were extremely religious men but their religion was largely on the outside. It was ostentatious and lacked sincerity. It did not spring from the heart. Such praying was aimed at receiving men's approval, not God's, and the praise of men was its only reward.

Jesus gave his disciples a second warning:

> 'In your prayers do not go babbling on like the heathen, who imagine that the more they say the more likely they are to be heard' (v. 7 NEB).

Prayer is not a routine activity, simply a matter of repeating and multiplying words. That is how the heathen pray, and such prayer is empty, formal, meaningless. 'Do not imitate them,' says Jesus. 'Your Father knows what your needs are before you ask him' (v. 8 NEB).

Nevertheless, although the Father already knows our needs, he still wishes us to pray, for in so doing we are acknowledging the place he ought to have in our lives and admitting our dependence on him. And therefore Jesus gave us the pattern prayer, to show us how to pray.

What he is insisting on is *reality* in prayer. When we pray we are not simply talking to ourselves, or parading our piety before others. We are communing with God; and God requires truth in the inward parts. The prayer he delights in is simple and sincere, and it need not be long-winded. Indeed one of the features of the Lord's Prayer is its brevity. It consists of less than sixty words. That fact should be an encouragement to those of us (and it is probably most of us) who find it difficult to pray at length. We need not be worried. What matters is not the length but the strength of our prayers: whether our hearts are in our praying and we are really in touch with God, or whether we are merely repeating a formula and engaging in a religious exercise.

For all its brevity and simplicity, the Lord's Prayer is remarkably comprehensive. It embraces all that ultimately matters in regard to God and man, things heavenly and earthly, our spiritual and material needs, the past, the present and the future. In its own way the prayer is perfect and complete, at once simple and profound. It is the prayer of the whole people of God, in every place, in every age.

The structure of the prayer is quite clear. After the opening invocation or address, 'Our Father, who art in heaven', it falls into two parts. The first is concerned entirely with God and his glory. We pray that his name may be hallowed, his kingdom come, and his will be done – in each instance on earth as in heaven. Quite deliberately and properly the prayer puts God first. It teaches us to focus our attention on him and to put his interests before our own.

The second part is concerned with man and his need – the whole of his need, physical, spiritual and moral. Just as the previous words are a revelation of God, so the words here are a picture of man, revealing his creatureliness, his sinfulness, and his weakness. Accordingly in the three brief petitions we ask God to supply each day our material necessities, to forgive our past sins and failures, and to safeguard our way ahead amid the temptations of the world, the flesh and the devil.

The final doxology is not part of the prayer as Jesus gave it, as modern translations of the New Testament make clear. It is an ascription of praise to God, derived from 1 Chronicles 29.11, and was added by the Church at a very early date to give the prayer a suitable liturgical ending.

We may look at the Lord's Prayer in another and less formal way. It can be regarded as a series of word-pictures illustrating our relationship with God, as follows:

The loving child – *Our Father, who art in heaven.*
The devout worshipper – *Hallowed be thy name.*
The loyal citizen – *Thy kingdom come.*
The obedient servant – *Thy will be done.*
The needy beggar – *Give us this day our daily bread.*
The discharged debtor – *Forgive us our trespasses* (or *debts*).
The vigilant pilgrim – *Lead us not into temptation.*
The liberated captive – *Deliver us from evil.*

Our Father in Heaven

Our Father, who art in heaven,
hallowed be thy name.

The key to the Lord's Prayer is found in its opening word; and the opening word, in the Greek as in the Latin, is *Father*. That word at once establishes a personal relationship between ourselves and God. If God is our Father, then we are his children; and if we are his children, then the rest of the prayer falls into place and everything makes sense.

When we begin to pray, the most important thing is to have a right image or picture of God in our minds. That must be obvious; for how we pray to him will depend on how we think of him. If our idea of him is wrong we cannot possibly pray to him aright.

Jesus teaches us to think of God as Father. That is the characteristic word which he himself used when speaking of God, and speaking to him. God is not simply the Ultimate Reality, the First Cause, the One Above, or some other abstract idea. He is the Father – *our* Father. He loves us. He created us. But above all he redeemed us; for the Christian doctrine of the Fatherhood of God rests not on the fact of creation but on the fact of redemption.

In a general sense it is true, of course, that God is the Father of all men, because he made all men and all men owe their existence to him. That is as far as *natural* religion takes us. But the New Testament revelation raises the subject to a supernatural level. In a particular sense God is the Father of those who have been drawn into a spiritual relationship with him through faith in the crucified and risen Saviour and have become his children by adoption and grace. The Fatherhood of God is bound up with the family of God, the Church of Jesus Christ. It is as members of the Christian family, and not merely of the human family, that we lift our hearts to God in prayer and say 'Our Father'.

The Aramaic word for father, *abba*, is an intimate, affectionate word. It is the word by which a Jewish child would address his father in the home circle. This is the word we use, the picture we have in mind, when we pray to God. The Spirit of Christ within us bears witness that we are God's children by crying 'Abba! Father!' (Romans 8.15; Galatians 4.6).

This means that as his children we can come to God with boldness and confidence and trust him to give us and do for us all that is for our good. And it means that we can talk to him in a perfectly natural way. We haven't got to employ a special language, some sort of high-flown religious jargon, when we pray. Nor is it necessary to pray in any special place or at any special hour. Every place is hallowed ground and every hour is sacred. We can speak to our Father anywhere, at any time – and about anything, however small or trivial. Remember, our little things are all big to God's love; our big things are all small to his power.

God is our Father: so Jesus teaches us. But he also asks us to remember that he is our Father *in heaven*, and these last two words must not be overlooked. They are a Jewish phrase, to be interpreted symbolically, not literally as though God were above the bright blue sky. They tell us not where God is but what he is. They affirm his *transcendence*: his greatness and glory, his perfection and power. The Father to whom we pray is, in the words of the Te Deum, 'the Father of an infinite majesty'.

This gives us a big conception of God. 'Great is the Lord, and highly to be praised!' cried the psalmist (48.1), and we should echo his words. So often our God is too small. We must beware of trivializing him, of cutting him down to our size as though he were such a one as ourselves. We must likewise beware of nationalizing him, as though he were simply the 'God of our fathers, known of old' and not Lord of all the earth. In the words of one of the Puritan divines, let us learn to think magnificently of God!

What bearing has this on our praying? Two answers suggest themselves. First, the thought of God's transcendence should impart confidence to our prayers. If when we pray we are really in touch with the Infinite, we may expect something to happen, for he is able to do far more than either we ask or think. Secondly, the thought of God's transcendence should impart a sense of reverence to our prayers. Our heavenly Father is also our King and our

Judge. So when we pray to him intimacy must be blended with humility, boldness with reverence. There is certainly no place for familiarity or sentimentality.

> If you say 'our Father' to the One who judges every man impartially on the record of his deeds, you must stand in awe of him while you live out your time on earth (1 Peter 1.17 NEB).

In keeping with this, the first petition in the Lord's Prayer is *Hallowed be thy name*. The 'name' in Scripture stands for the person. God's name is God himself as he has revealed himself to us. The Greek verb translated 'hallowed' comes from the word *hagios*, holy, and means to treat as sacred, to honour, to revere.

This first petition is therefore a recognition of the holiness of God. It is virtually an act of worship. It compels us at the outset of our praying to bow before our heavenly Father in homage and adoration and cry:

> Holy, Holy, Holy, Lord God of hosts!
> Heaven and earth are full of thy glory,
> Glory be to thee, O Lord most high.

As we thus hallow God's name in our own hearts and lives, our longing must be that all men and nations should do the same. This is the purpose of the prayer. We are asking that everyone, everywhere, may worship and magnify the all-holy God and ascribe to him the honour, glory and praise which his character demands and deserves.

We said at the beginning of this chapter that how we pray to God will depend on how we think of him. Jesus tells us in these opening words of the prayer to think of his fatherhood, his transcendence, his holiness. If we do so, we shall pray accordingly: with confidence, with humility, and with reverence.

The Kingdom of God

Thy kingdom come,
thy will be done,
on earth as it is in heaven.

What is meant by the kingdom of God? And why should we pray for its coming? Unless we are clear about the answer to those questions we cannot offer this prayer with any serious intention.

Biblical scholars have written whole volumes examining and expounding the kingdom of God (or kingdom of heaven: the phrases are synonymous) and in the process they have tended to complicate rather than clarify the subject. We might well get the impression that the whole thing is very difficult to understand. Yet it cannot really be so difficult, for Jesus himself was constantly talking about the kingdom, and talking about it not to religious experts but to quite ordinary people like ourselves. So what did *he* mean when he spoke of God's kingdom?

On one point at least scholars are now generally agreed. The basic idea of the Greek word *basileia* is the rule or reign of God. 'It is not so much a place over which God rules as God's reign itself' (Alan Richardson). To put it quite simply, the kingdom of God is the kingship of God, the exercise of his kingly rule in human life and society. It expresses the way in which the life of mankind ought to be ordered – and must be ordered, if it is to make sense – namely, in submission to God's grace and sovereignty.

The prayer *Thy kingdom come* is thus a prayer which acknowledges that the Lord is King, the rightful King of all men. His kingship is a present reality. In a true sense the kingdom of God has already come. It came with the coming of Jesus to this world. In his own person he embodied the kingdom, for his life was totally subject to God's rule. By his redemptive work, his cross and resurrection and outpouring of the Spirit, he inaugurated the kingdom: he opened the kingdom of heaven to all who believe in him, as the Te Deum proclaims.

So the kingdom of God is here now, as a divine act and a divine gift. In the words of A. M. Hunter:

> It is the sovereign saving activity of God. It is his reign becoming manifestly effective in the world of human experience. It is God in action, God in conflict with evil, through Jesus, for man's salvation.[1]

When we pray for the *coming* of God's kingdom we are asking that his saving rule may become operative on an ever increasing scale in the world of today. For while it is true that God is the rightful king of all men, it is equally true that all men do not want him to rule their lives. They want to be independent of God and to rule their own lives. Jesus pictured this in his parable of the nobleman who went into a far country to be appointed king and then return. But in his absence his fellow citizens rebelled and declared, 'We do not want this man as our king' (Luke 19.12–14).

It is like that in our modern world. And that is why the world is in such a mess. It is not subject to the rule of God. Men are in rebellion against his government. They are trying to run the world in their own way, not his. They think they can manage without God. The result is evident for all to see.

One thing now becomes plain. The kingdom of God is not just a 'religious' matter or a piece of abstract theology. It is something intensely practical. It has a direct bearing on our political life, on the way our society is run. It is also a very personal matter. If society is to be changed, people must first be changed. As William Barclay remarks, the kingdom of God must come in the hearts of men before it can even begin to come in the world at large.

This means that the kingdom now finds its expression in the lives of those who acknowledge the lordship of Christ and submit themselves to him; and that is simply another way of saying that the Church is the present *embodiment* of the kingdom. The Church is not to be identified with the kingdom; nevertheless it is the area of human life where the kingdom finds, or should find, visible expression.

And something more. The Church is also the *instrument* of the kingdom, the means by which God extends his kingly rule among mankind. So 'Thy kingdom come' is a missionary prayer. It recognizes that the initiative lies with God, not with us. We cannot 'bring in' the kingdom by our own efforts. But the prayer also implies that we are prepared to share with God in the work of the kingdom and to play our part in the Church's mission to preach the gospel of the kingdom throughout the world, until the consummation of the kingdom at the end of the age (Matthew 24.14).

The purpose behind our prayer for the coming of God's kingdom is made clear in the petition that follows: *thy will be done, on earth as it is in heaven*. Rightly understood, what a glorious petition this is! It is not a sigh of resignation but a cry of glad and positive assent. For the will of God is not a burden grievous to be borne. It is all that is good and pleasing and perfect in God's sight (Romans 12.2); and therefore his will is justice, truth, compassion, peace, purity, and health.

That being so, let us be clear that there is nothing better for us and for our world than that God's will should be done. All around us we see so much that is wrong: injustice, brutality, tyranny, intolerance, bloodshed, poverty, disease, suffering. Why is it? It is because man's will is done, not God's. And when we confront these evil things and in Christ's name pray to the Father 'Thy will be done', we are not asking for patience to accept them but for courage to fight and vanquish them. For it is not God's will that these things should abide. It is his will that they should be abolished. And he wants us, who own his kingly rule, to co-operate with him in doing his will, so making this earth a different and a better place.

Note

[1] *The Work and Words of Jesus* (SCM Press, 1950), p. 76.

Body and Soul

Give us this day our daily bread;
and forgive us our trespasses,
as we forgive those who trespass against us.

The Lord's Prayer, as we have seen, puts God first and begins with the things that concern his glory. The second part, to which we now turn, complements this and takes up the subject of our human needs. Dr Alexander Maclaren pointed out that the two parts of the prayer follow a different sequence of thought. The first part starts at the highest point, with our Father in heaven, and comes down to the level of earth. In the second part the movement is reversed. Beginning on the material level, it rises to the spiritual and reaches it climax in deliverance from evil.

In the prayer *Give us this day our daily bread*, Jesus was teaching us to commit to God our temporal, bodily needs and to live a day at a time. The word 'bread' of course is symbolical and inclusive. It covers the whole of the material side of life, all that has to do with our physical well-being. In Martin Luther's catechism the prayer is explained thus:

> I mean by it everything belonging to the want and supply of our life; that is, food, drink, clothes, dwelling, gardens, lands, flocks, money, happy marriage, virtuous children, faithful servants, just magistrates, peaceful government, wholesome air, quietness, health, true friends, faithful neighbours, and such like things.

Perhaps Luther was going a bit too far. The prayer entitles us to pray for necessities, but not for luxuries. But he had got the right idea in giving the word bread this bigger and wider sense. It is surely our heavenly Father's intention that his children should live a rich and full life in this world of bounty in which he has placed them. We may be certain from our Lord's teaching (e.g. Matthew 6.23–34) that he cares for our bodily needs and is ready to supply them.

In praying for our daily bread we acknowledge our ultimate dependence on God for everything we have. We are not self-sufficient, as we are sometimes tempted to imagine. We can (and must) co-operate with God in the ordering of our lives, but we cannot control him. In the end it remains true that all good gifts around us are sent from heaven above.

We pray for *our* daily bread. It is not a selfish prayer. As Christ's disciples we remember the needs of others; and it is more than ever essential that we should do so today when we for our part have more than enough, while a large area of humanity is impoverished and undernourished. In our praying as well as in our giving we must involve ourselves with the hungry, the helpless, and the hopeless. God cares for them. So should we.

But we must go further. Man has other requirements than daily bread and all that that implies. The prayer continues: *and forgive us our trespasses*; for just as we have need of daily food, so we have need of daily forgiveness.

'Give us . . . and forgive us . . .' The two petitions bring into immediate association the two fundamental aspects of life, the physical and the spiritual. Man is both body and soul. He is not simply a physical being with very real bodily needs. He is also and above all a spiritual being, made in the image of God, made for communion with God; and it is only in communion with God that he fulfils himself and becomes the sort of person he is intended to be.

This is where forgiveness comes in. Fellowship with God is impossible without his forgiveness. Sin breaks the harmony between us. Until we are forgiven we cannot know God's peace in our hearts or his presence in our lives. We cannot have a tranquil mind or a clear conscience.

How can we find forgiveness? We cannot earn it. We can only receive it through the mercy of God and the cross of our Lord Jesus Christ. And here we should note that in the biblical version of the Lord's Prayer the correct translation of the phrase 'forgive us our trespasses' is 'forgive us our *debts*' (Matthew 6.12). The phrase serves to remind us that we come to God as bankrupt sinners who owe God everything and have nothing to pay. We owe him our obedience, our love, our loyalty, our worship, our service; but we hopelessly fail to meet our obligations. Nothing on our part can wipe out the debt we owe. Only God can remit it; and he does so as a sheer act of grace for Christ's sake. The debt we cannot pay has been paid for us. This is part at least of what we mean by the Atonement. We can only pray, 'Father, forgive us our debts', because of what Christ has done for us, because of the price he paid for our salvation (see, e.g., Mark 10.45; 1 Corinthians 6.19, 20; 1 Peter 1.18, 19; Revelation 5.9).

Sinners as we are, God's full and free forgiveness is available to us in Christ – *if* we are ready to receive it. For there is a condition attached: 'Forgive us our trespasses, *as we forgive those who trespass against us*.' It has been rightly said that 'unforgiving, unforgiven' is a law of the kingdom of God. He offers his forgiveness to *penitent* sinners. An unforgiving spirit is an impenitent spirit. If then we are unforgiving we exclude ourselves from the forgiveness of God.

The words Jesus added at the end of the prayer explain this: 'If you forgive men their trespasses, your heavenly Father also will forgive you; but if you do not forgive men their trespasses, neither will your Father forgive your trespasses' (Matthew 6.14, 15). The parable of the unforgiving servant, or unmerciful debtor, in Matthew 18.23–35 provides an excellent illustration. But let us be clear that there is no question of human merit in this matter. We do not forgive others in order to receive God's forgiveness. We forgive them because we *have* received his forgiveness. St Paul's words sum it all up: 'Be kind to one another, tenderhearted, forgiving one another, as God in Christ forgave you' (Ephesians 4.32).

Temptation and Evil

Lead us not into temptation,
but deliver us from evil.

The petition 'give us this day our daily bread' recognizes our present needs. 'Forgive us our trespasses' has to do with our past offences. The petition that follows and which concludes the prayer takes account of our future path.

We have asked God to pardon our sins, and if we have asked aright we may be sure that he has granted our petition. But when we have received God's forgiveness we have not finished with sin, nor has sin finished with us. Never in this life are we 'saved to sin no more'. As long as we live we are sinners and sin remains in us. It is the honest acceptance of this state of affairs that prompts us to pray, *Lead us not into temptation*.

Many Christians are puzzled by this petition, or at least by the way it is phrased. They ask, 'Is it likely that God would deliberately lead his people into temptation? Is he not too good and wise a Father to do that? Why then do we ask him not to do so?'

The words obviously call for some clarification. Many of the early Church fathers interpreted the prayer as meaning, 'Do not allow us to be led into temptation.' St Augustine stated that in his day the prayer was commonly used in this form. Some two centuries earlier Origen, the great Alexandrian biblical scholar, commented: 'We should pray not that we may not be tempted, which is impossible, but that we may not be brought under the power of temptation.'

There is a vast difference between being subjected to temptation and being subdued by it. Temptation is a simple fact of life and cannot be evaded. No one is immune from it (1 Corinthians 10.13). And since in the Bible the word often has the meaning of *testing*, temptation can serve a good purpose in God's providence. The trials we encounter in life not only test the quality of our faith; they also purify and strengthen it and produce maturity of character (see 1 Peter 1.6, 7; James 1.2; Romans 5.3, 4).

To be tempted is one thing. To yield to it is another. The hymn some of us used to sing in earlier life,

> Yield not to temptation,
> For yielding is sin,

states an important truth. Temptation is not sin. Jesus was tempted in the same manner as we are and yet was without sin. Surely what we are really asking, when we pray that God will not lead us into temptation, is that we may be kept from sinning. In that sense the prayer is almost identical with that in the third collect of Morning Prayer in the BCP: 'Grant that this day we fall into no sin'. This is what our Lord meant when in the Garden of Gethsemane he told his disciples, 'Pray that you may not enter into temptation' (it is the same word, *peirasmos*, as in the Lord's Prayer). He well knew the danger that confronted them at that moment. They would not be spared temptation, nor would he. For them as for himself it was a testing hour. *He* faced his temptation with earnest prayer to the Father and won the battle. He was urging his disciples to do the same.

In using this petition we are both facing the fact of temptation and confessing our own weakness, our liability to fail. At the same time we are undertaking not to court danger and lead ourselves into temptation. To do that would be to make a mockery of the prayer. Just because we are so weak, we cast ourselves upon God's grace and ask him to guard us in time of spiritual peril – and to *deliver us from evil*.

With this great cry for liberation the Lord's Prayer reaches its climax. The word 'evil' may also be translated 'evil one', as in the NEB ('save us from the evil one'). But which ever translation we adopt, there is no denying that evil is one of the greatest realities in life as well as one of its deepest mysteries.

We meet with evil in many different forms. There is evil within our own hearts, in our fallen human nature. There is evil around us in the 'world', in the Bible sense of society organized apart from God. There is evil in the shape of unjust and tyrannical government: evil regimes that hold life cheap and disregard human rights. There are evil men who inflict suffering on others by crime, violence, terrorism, torture. There are social and political evils such as world poverty, racial discrimination, religious intolerance, prostitution, the degradation of sex. There is evil in the form of sickness, revealing itself in diseased bodies and darkened minds. There is evil in the intellectual sphere, evil which manifests itself in ignorance, falsehood and error. And with all this, and behind all this, is the evil one himself, the devil or Satan, the 'malignant personal power, himself wholly evil, and the source of evil to others' (C. F. Evans). Well may we cry to God our Father, 'Deliver us from evil! Save us from the evil one!'

One thing stands out very clearly. Jesus took the problem of sin and evil extremely seriously. He recognized that sin is man's greatest enemy and that deliverance from evil is man's biggest need. Two out of the three petitions in the second part of the prayer are occupied with the subject. This amounts to a third of the prayer as a whole.

We dare not think lightly of sin, or excuse it, or explain it away. If we are true to the Lord who gave us this prayer we must continually, as needy penitent sinners, pray for God's forgiveness, ask for grace to be saved from sinning, and seek liberation from the power of evil in all its diabolical forms.

Saying the Lord's Prayer

Are we to regard the Lord's Prayer as a form of prayer, or as a pattern of prayer?

In St Luke's Gospel it is given as a form: 'When you pray, say . . .' In St Matthew it is offered as a pattern: 'This is how you should pray . . .' (Luke 11.2; Matthew 6.9). Hence the answer to our question is that the prayer is to be regarded both as a form and as a pattern.

It is inevitable, and wholly right, that it should be adopted as a form of prayer, for it comes from Jesus himself and bears his own imprimatur. For the same reason it has the great advantage of being a prayer which is common to all Christian people and is a uniting factor among the different churches. It is a form of prayer which expresses the mind of Christ and which therefore we can offer with confidence in his name.

Nevertheless, the use of any form of prayer has its dangers, particularly the danger of our simply repeating the words without realizing or meaning what we say. The words may be on our lips but not in our hearts. It is all the more needful for us to be on our guard against this in the case of the Lord's Prayer, for in giving it to his disciples he said (as the AV puts it), 'When ye pray, use not vain repetitions, as the heathen do'. The frequent saying of the Lord's Prayer can easily become a vain repetition, a series of 'pattered Paternosters'.

How are we to guard against this danger? It would obviously help if we were to say the prayer more slowly than we normally do in public worship; to think about the words as we repeat them, and to have a clear understanding of what they mean. There are words and phrases, as we have noted, which require some explanation, such as 'in heaven', 'hallowed', 'kingdom', 'our daily bread', 'temptation'.

The purpose of these short studies has been to make the prayer more intelligible and therefore more realistic and more relevant. We must try to put ourselves, so to speak, into the prayer as we say it and apply it to our own lives and circumstances. What is everybody's prayer must become *our* prayer. What is a prayer for every age must become a prayer for today.

The prayer, however, is more than a set of words for constant repetition. It is a pattern of prayer. It offers us a guide as to *how* to pray, and this is the really important thing. The spirit of prayer matters far more than the language of prayer. It matters more than the method we employ, or the time and place we choose, or the posture we adopt.

The Lord's Prayer has a lot to teach us about the spirit of prayer. Take some illustrations.

We come to God in a *filial* spirit, addressing him as our Father since we are his children by adoption and grace.

We come in a *humble* spirit, bowing before him as the high and holy One who inhabits eternity.

We come in an *obedient* spirit, submitting ourselves to his kingly rule and ready to serve his will on earth.

We come in a *dependent* spirit, looking to him to care for all our daily bodily needs.

We come in a *penitent* spirit, acknowledging our sins and seeking his forgiveness, even as we have forgiven others.

We come in a *trustful* spirit, resting our weakness on his strength and asking him to guard us from sinning and rescue us from evil.

It is clear that we cannot be content merely with saying the Lord's Prayer. It is a simple matter to say it. It is much more difficult to *pray* it – and to pray it sincerely, honestly, and meaningfully. For in this prayer we are not only making big demands on God. We are also making considerable demands upon ourselves. In the words we repeat so often there is a challenge which closely touches our lives.

Many years ago I came across a short article entitled 'Can you say the Lord's Prayer?' written by M. W. Gass. With grateful acknowledgements I reproduce the substance of it here, slightly amended in places.

> I cannot say *Our* if I live in a watertight spiritual compartment and think only of myself.

I cannot say *Father* if I do not demonstrate the relationship in my daily life.

I cannot say *Who art in heaven* if I do not bow in reverence before the Almighty.

I cannot say *Hallowed be thy name* if I, who am called by his name, am not holy.

I cannot say *Thy kingdom come* if I am not doing all in my power to hasten its coming.

I cannot say *Thy will be done* if I am questioning, resentful of or disobedient to his will for me.

I cannot say *Give us this day our daily bread* if I am lazy and not prepared to earn my daily living.

I cannot say *Forgive us our trespasses, as we forgive those who trespass against us*, if I harbour a grudge against anyone.

I cannot say *Lead us not into temptation* if I deliberately place myself in a position where I am likely to be tempted.

I cannot say *Deliver us from evil* if I am not prepared to fight it in the spiritual realm with the weapon of prayer.

I cannot say *Amen* if I do not also add 'Cost what it may.' For to say this prayer honestly will cost everything.